HOPE *Always* WINS

15 Days to Strong

HOPE *Always* WINS

15 Days to Strong

MARLA LUCAS

Xulon Press
2301 Lucien Way #415
Maitland, FL 32751
407.339.4217
www.xulonpress.com

Special thanks to editor:
Heather Van Allen
hlvanallen23@gmail.com

Paperback ISBN-13: 978-1-66282-930-7
Ebook ISBN-13: 978-1-66282-931-4

GOD'S GIFTS OF HOPE TO ME...

Stephen and Christian. Words fall short to express how much I love you. You both share hope every day with every person you meet, but especially me. I love watching God open so many doors for both of you to make this world a better place. From the moment you were born, you inspired me to keeping hoping even on my hardest days.

Stephen, you are my baby boy who gave me the best name on the planet, mama. I love your heart to take care of everyone on your path; your family (especially Grandma), your friends and even total strangers who need a hand. You are always the first to rescue. Your humble heart to go out of your way to help others over your own needs reminds me of God's great love.

Christian, what a joy it is to watch you live your best life inspiring others to never give up and never be afraid to think and believe for a BIG life. I love your strength and commitment to excellence. I love your brave and kind heart that gives God all the credit for your successes.

You boys are the light of my life. I thank God for every beautiful, adventurous day we've been blessed to live. I'm beyond blessed that God would give me two world-changing sons, like you.

I couldn't love you more or be any more proud of you,

Mom

TABLE OF CONTENTS

Introduction

hope (noun) - An expectation and desire for
a certain positive outcome to happen.

Hope. This one word can make your whole life incredibly exhilarating and passionate, or the lack of it can wear you down to questioning why you're even here. Why do some people have it and others long for it?

Recent studies show that an alarming number of people are feeling hopeless.[1] The effects and responses to hopelessness showed more harmful outcomes than that of depression. This is not God's plan for His creation. John 10:10 (ESV) says, "The thief comes only to steal and kill and destroy. I came that they may have life and have it abundantly." God's desire is that we have an abundant life. The urgency to share hope gets me up in the morning. This one thing I know — hope fuels our future.

I love to fly. From packing to the plane ride, I love it all. I start making my packing list a month ahead of time. I plan out all of my outfits for each day. I carefully go over my list to see which items I can wear twice so everything fits in my little luggage. Then, I check my list off as I pack. This is a serious process for a planner, like moi'.

The day finally comes. I have planned and organized until the wee hours. I've lost sleep dreaming of this vacation. I love all of it, the restaurants at the airport, the snacks onboard, reading my favorite magazine, watching the people, and taking in the scenery. The moment is finally here. I'm boarding the plane for the vacation of a lifetime.

Imagine that level of excitement and finally boarding, only to hear the pilot announce, "I'm sorry, you'll have to exit the plane; we have no fuel. This plane is not going anywhere." It doesn't matter how awesome the plane is, how much preparing I have done for this amazing vacation. Without fuel, I'm not leaving the airport. The same is true with our lives. We can talk about our callings, goals, and dreams all day, but we need the empowering fuel of "hope" to fly that plane.

You were magnificently created in God's image with gifts and talents you've barely tapped into. You have a vision, a dream, places you want to go, people you want to reach, God-given goals you want to achieve. Hope is the fuel to move you into your calling and your next adventurous season of life. Hope — and a few power moves — will get you where you want to go.

You and I are responsible for filling our own fuel tanks. It's not difficult, but it must be intentional. We are not getting off this plane. With God's help and His Word, we are filling up the fuel tank. You've worked too hard to get here. You just need a plan for takeoff. "If people can't see what God is doing, they stumble all over themselves; but when they attend to what he reveals, they are most blessed" (Proverbs 29:18, MSG). It's time to "attend" to what God has revealed. He has given you incredibly unique gifts. He has put dreams in your heart. It's time to hit the GO button. Hope will get you going and take you to your next beautiful destination. Hope will remind you that every day is another opportunity to watch God work through you to accomplish feats way beyond your imagination.

Specific habits of hope have transformed my life. When I have unshakeable hope in God, there is no question I live life on a different plain. How do I know these power moves work? I did the work. I have spent the last 20-plus years educating myself, reading and studying God's Word and human behavior. I have come to the conclusion that when a person chooses to hope in God, strength is inevitable.

I don't believe in coincidences. God orchestrates meetings, and this book, right now, has provided one of those meetings. I believe God put us together to experience His hope — empowering hope — and live a victorious life consecrated in Him. There is not one other person with the unique influence and gifts that you have. Not one. You have a job to do.

Perhaps you have an incredible marriage, or you just found yourself single again. Maybe you have 10 children or no children. Maybe you just lost your job or you just landed your dream job. Wherever you are on this magnificent journey, you were "created for such a time as this" (Esther 4:14). More than one Scripture tells us that God had a plan while we were still in the womb. "Before I formed you in the womb, I knew you" (Jeremiah 1:5). In the womb, God knew everything about you. He knows your heart. He knows your strengths and weaknesses. He knows what inspires you. He loves new beginnings. He loves you.

Through triumphs and tragedies, we become who we are today. In Ex 50:20, Joseph said, "You intended to harm me, but God intended it all for good. He brought me to this position so I could save the lives of many people." Just like you, I've been through my share of "Oh Yay!" and "Oh No!" life events.

Daddy always said, "Whatever you look for, that is what you'll find." I think that may be one of the most profound statements ever said about hope. Are you looking for it? How do you find it? How do you keep it? Wherever you are on your journey, it's time to take steps to run after the dreams God has put in your heart. God has given us resources to hope again. We've got things to do. The future is too incredible to look back even one more day.

Starting this minute, we are taking giant steps and making new decisions. You have made it through some rough waters.

Your hard stuff is different from my hard stuff, but we all have hard stuff. God has been there. He's still there, but not just so you can barely survive. This life it too short. It's time to live this beautiful life on a new level, it's time to level-up!

I've been asked several times: Is there a pill or a certain vitamin that you take that keeps you consistently hopeful and joyful? and How in the world are you so happy when I know your life has been hard? I do have very specific ways that I navigate hardship. I'm sharing some of the tangible actions that I take to keep my focus through the ups and downs of this always-changing ride called life. I'm going to share with you how I maneuver life-changes, especially the hard ones. My prayer is that God will reveal truth that will empower and strengthen you.

Invite a friend. Your life is about to change drastically, bringing someone along will make you both stronger. We all need accountability and encouragement. Reading this book with a friend will maximize your efforts. Maybe you know someone who needs hope, or you want to lock arms with someone you love and make a fresh start at living again. Whatever your circumstances may be at this moment, it's time to love your life...crazy-awesome miracles are on the other side of HOPE.

This journey is not about finding time; it's about making time to implement changes and hope again! You're doing the most important work of your life. You're building a healthy and hope-filled you. I couldn't be more honored to join you on your expedition. Hold on tight, hold on to God, trust His plan, and let's get busy.

I'm thankful for breathtaking, awesomely-wonderful moments and I'm thankful for moments of deep sorrow, because God uses it all. Miscarrying my first baby, going through a house fire, divorcing after 20 years, navigating incredibly scary career changes, losing my amazing father, and facing that surprise battle with cancer, God was there. Every step of the way He was there — and He is with you, too. Even when it doesn't feel like it, He's there.

We have everything we need to overcome and hope again. "In all things we are more than conquerors through Him who loved us" (Romans 8:37).

Buckle up buttercup! Life is about to get exciting, and we're going places. I'd like to invite you to jump on this hope-filled plane with me. An incredible destination awaits us. How do I know this? Because you're reading this book, and "HOPE ALWAYS WINS."

Day 1

THIRTY MINUTES

Time spent alone with God is never wasted.

Fifteen days. That's fast. In order for a 15-day transformation to happen, you have to be all-in. You can do this. A power move is a big bold step moving you in the direction you want to go with your life. I'm not leaving you guessing what those power moves should be. I'm sharing the most important power moves you can make to change your life forever, because they will immediately move you in the right direction in order to accomplish your dreams.

The mission: be brave, make decisions, and take action steps that lead to a powerful, hope-filled life. No one wants to spend their entire life searching for a way to make it better. In the next 15 days, you can make major moves that will change the trajectory of your life. The reason I know this – I did it.

A power move for Noah was hammering the first nail to build the ark when there was no rain nor had there ever been. A power move for David was walking out to meet Goliath with five stones and a slingshot. A power move for Esther was risking her life to go before the king without being summoned. A power move for Ruth was leaving everything she had known to follow her mother-in-law. I love all of those power moves, but those moves were all secondary to the very first power move every one of those heroes made.

To say that nothing else, not one single thing, will change your life as much as this one habit, would be an understatement. This first power move will change your life the very minute you establish it. The moment you add this habit to your life, you will never go back to business as usual. Your life will never be the same. Nothing is as great a priority nor results in as great a return on your investment.

The absolute #1 life-changing habit is a daily, designated, intentional time set aside for God.

When you commit to deliberately seek God and make the very first power move that Noah, David, Esther, and Ruth implemented, you will see the kind of results they saw. This is the first action step to hope. It's the first power move I made, and it's the singular most important intentional habit that can be established in your life. I'm not asking for the moon here people. It's 30 minutes. Thirty minutes that will guarantee your life will never be the same.

Be prepared. The enemy of our souls will not like this plan. He will attack your plan. He will not take this lying down. Every minute you spend with God is another minute you are getting stronger and he loses power in your life. He will tempt you to procrastinate until your day is gone. He will remind you of hundreds of very important things that need to be done instead. Fight back! This sacred time is a non-negotiable time set aside every day for prayer and power in your life. Here is why it is the greatest and most important power move you can make in your life: "Call to me and I will answer you, and will tell you great and hidden things that you have not known" (Jeremiah 33:3, ESV). This is a commitment to hear from the Creator of the universe. This is time set aside to find out hidden things that you did not know before. In order to transform your life, this power move must take place, and it must be your first move. Watch and journal the miracles that will begin happening in your life the moment you implement this habit. It will rock your world.

A word of warning: everything under the sun will try to keep you from this time with God. My power move started with 30 minutes every day. I decided there is absolutely no reason I couldn't commit to 30 minutes a day, and it changed my life. Once you establish this habit, you will look forward to it. It will be the highlight of your day, as you make your requests known and watch for the answers. "Do not be anxious about anything, but in every situation, by prayer and petition, with thanksgiving, present your requests to God" (Philippians 4:6). This time with God will look like this: pray, petition, give thanks, present. From the very first day you make this power move, God will move in your situation. I promise (because He promised).

I set a reminder on my phone so that I get a notification every evening. If I say that God is my priority, my schedule should reflect that. My relationship with God is the most powerful and important of all my relationships. If I'm not careful, it easily becomes second, third, or Oh, good grief! I haven't spent time with God; no wonder I'm feeling lost. I decided to set a timer and focus in on God without checking the clock. My goal was to keep praying until my timer went off. I wanted to train myself to engage in prayer for a solid 30 minutes, to be all-in during my prayer time, not allowing my mind to wander. Disciplining myself to be still in God's presence and listen to His voice. I was learning the power of intentional time with God. It is during these times, He will speak. He will give us good ideas. He will give us another perspective. He will encourage us not to give up. Your time with God will become your favorite life-changing time of the day.

Thirty minutes building a relationship? A relationship with God works like any relationship. The more time you spend with Him, the better you will know Him. You will recognize His voice throughout your day. You will make better decisions when God is your first go-to for help. You will hear Him speak to your heart more often. You will build a better life as you spend consecrated time with Him every day and He reveals hidden things to you.

Even when you don't feel like it — or better yet — especially when you don't feel like it, make sure you spend this alone time with God. Start today, not tomorrow, even if it's 5 or 10 minutes. This is the one habit that will bring more desired outcomes than all other habits combined. Your most significant changes will take place when this habit is implemented. This time is not leftover time in your day. It is intentional time faithfully seeking God and His plan for your life, so that you live your best life.

Seek God for divine wisdom. Chatting with friends about your life, you will get friend input that comes with limited knowledge and an inability to fully see every facet of your situation. Call your friends to pray with you, not to solve your problems. I have friends that I call on for prayer. "Again, truly I tell you that if two of you on earth agree about anything they ask for, it will be done for them by my Father in heaven. For where two or three gather in my name, there am I with them"

(Matthew 18:19-2). My friends and I go on prayer walks, we go on prayer treadmills, and you may even see us on prayer-mall-walks (not kidding). At the very least, we pray on the phone. God loves when people pray together, which makes me want to pray with friends. "Prayer friends, party of two or three, your table is ready!" I'm in. Let's pray! Fun is when God answers a prayer, and you get to tell your friend who prayed with you (and remembers when you had nearly lost all hope). Together you get to see how God answered your prayer next-level. God loves prayer partners.

When you spend time with God, you hear from the all-knowing, all-powerful, all-present, Almighty God, who formed every blood vessel in your body. (Fact: if you lined up all of your adult-sized blood vessels they would extend 100,000 miles. Wow! Only God.[2]) Not only does God know your history, He knows what's coming next. He knows the way it's all going to go. Never spend more time getting advice or counsel from anyone on this planet than you spend listening to the One who created it all. Come on y'all, that's logic.

Prayer is communication with God. It's our means of building relationship with our Father. Prayer is personal. It's your private conversation with the One who created you and loves you more than anyone else. Sometimes I start with the Lord's Prayer, "Our Father in heaven, hallowed be your name, your kingdom come, your will be done, on earth as it is in heaven. Give us today our daily bread. And forgive us our debts, as we also have forgiven our debtors. And lead us not into temptation, but deliver us from the evil one" (Matthew 6:9-13). Other times, I start my prayer by thanking God for my many blessings, such as, my family, health, job, and friends. And then, there are the days my prayer goes like this:

> Oh, dear God! Help! Oh Mylanta! I need your help! I'm trying not to die from over-load here, Lord! I need you, and if you could intervene in the next five minutes, that would be so awesome! But I do trust your timing, Lord. But if you could help me not die from overwhelm — that would be so great!

God hears those prayers, too. God shows us how to pray. He tells us that He inhabits the praises of His people. Always include praise. We've been invited to "boldly" ask God for help. For every desperate situation, every need, every request, God wants to help. "Let us therefore come boldly unto the throne of grace, that we may obtain mercy, and find grace to help in time of need" (Hebrews 4:16, KJV). Mercy is on the way. Grace is on the way. Help is on the way. We obey God's Word, and He intervenes. It's that simple.

One particular night, I was praying and asking God for help in a certain situation. I thought He might tell me what to do next, but, nope. All I could sense was, "Do not fear." I wasn't expecting that. I stopped for a minute and I said, "Lord, I was really looking for a next-step kind of answer?" I sensed it again, "Do not fear." Then I realized that was my next step. God was telling me to take a deep breath; the answer would come in the perfect time — His time. My job right now was to rest, trust, and not fear. That's the kind of answer I'm talking about. He will give you direction, but you have to be quiet and still enough to hear Him. And, how about the fact that He is a whisper away, 24 hours a day, 7 days a week? That's powerful. One of my favorite Scriptures that has gotten me through many trials is Psalm 46:10, "Be still and know that I am God." Say it out loud and say it often. He will calm your turbulent seas and bring you indescribable hope.

A 24-Hour Miracle

God has answered so many prayers in our lives if we stop and think about it long enough. One miracle in particular was so crazy-cool. It happened overnight and was so specific it could only have been God. It all started with the movie, "War Room," with Priscilla Shirer. If you haven't seen the movie, you need to. It will change your life forever. It was all about a wife (Priscilla) on a journey to pray and save her family. She would go into her prayer closet and call out to God and, literally, her whole life turned around as God answered her prayers. One of my favorite scenes, maybe because it reminded me of something I would do, is the scene where Priscilla was trying to make her prayer closet comfy. She brought in pillows and chairs. She took her soda and snacks so she could munch when she got hungry. I mean, you'd think she was going to be in there for 6 months, not 30 minutes. I was cracking up.

There was a moment when her husband was about to fall into major sin. She had become aware of what was going on and went into her prayer closet and interceded for him. God intervened! Affair averted. Her husband came back home, the family was saved, and they went on to stay together and build a great life. Woo-hoo!

We all know life doesn't always happen the way the movie went. But what I do know is when you spend time interceding with God, He will be right there with you, He will help you, and He will act. It may not turn out exactly like the movie, but you're making your own box-office hit, God's way. The best way. Trust His way even when it looks a little different than you thought it would. It was fun to watch the movie depict an awesome miracle from start to finish in 120 minutes. I hope you get to see it. It will challenge you to create your own "war room."

That's what I did. I created my very own "war room." I watched the movie and felt inspired to be more intentional with my prayer time. I created my little "war room" in my tiny apartment, a place to seek God and ask for His divine intervention in some of the spiritual battles I was facing. I was doing battle for people I loved, my work, all things important to me.

Did I mention this prayer closet was in my teeny-weenie, tiny apartment? So, now you know how big my closet was. Yeah, I was squished between jeans and shirts. Sometimes I'd be praying and realize I was sitting on a shoe. Nice. My backside would start going numb and I'd have to make adjustments. I didn't care; I was on a mission. People I loved needed me. They needed my prayers. I was determined and not even my Manolo Blahniks could stop me! (Just kidding, Walmarte'. Perhaps you've heard of that designer?)

It was a Friday night. I went into my war room with a pen, sticky notes, and my Bible. I decided I would pray very specifically for a few needs in my life. I wrote down the names of both of my sons. As I was praying for one of them in particular, God prompted me to write the name of one of his friends on my sticky note, so I did. I began to pray semi-vague prayers about them coming to church and that the boys would hunger and thirst for righteousness. I looked at my note and decided to write "church" next to their names.

The interesting thing is that I had no idea where my son's friend was at the time. I didn't even know if he and my son still talked. It had been months and months since I had heard his name. And so, I kept praying for both boys. As I looked at my note that read "church," I felt like God was telling me to be more specific. I was thinking, If I leave this vague and he goes to church at some time in his life, that will be an answered prayer. But that was not what God wanted to show me. I felt Him tell me to specifically pray that the boys would be in church that Sunday. I had a little conversation with God. "Lord, are you sure? I mean this Sunday is two days away. I completely understand if you need a little more time. I mean, the last time I saw my son's friend, well, let's just say he wasn't attending Bible studies on a regular basis." God repeated Himself to me, "This Sunday."

I took the sticky note down off my wall and added, "THIS SUNDAY." Oh, my word, I had such a crazy feeling, like I just pressured the Almighty God. I thought about Hebrews 4:16 (NLT), telling us to "come boldly to the throne of our gracious God" and I began to pray, "Okay, Lord, I know this is bold, but I also know you can do absolutely anything. I'm asking you right now for my son and his friend to be in church this Sunday. You said to 'call unto you' in Jeremiah 33:3, and that's what I'm doing. I'm asking for a supernatural miracle."

I went to bed that Friday night. The next morning, I awoke and went to the kitchen. As I walked by the living room, I looked over and on my couch was my son AND HIS FRIEND, the very friend God told me to pray for the night before. I did a double-take. I couldn't believe my eyes. He looked at me and said, "Hi, Ms. Marla." I said, "Hey. What are you doing?" He said, "Well, I hung out with your son last night and he invited me to stay the night." I was speechless. I said, "Okay, I need you to hold on one minute." I hurried to my prayer closet, got the pink sticky note, and rushed back to the living room. I said, "I want you to see what I was praying last night. I was praying for YOU. God put you on my heart and told me to pray for you! I haven't seen you in probably a year! I just need to tell you, it's no accident you are at my house this morning."

We visited for a bit and then I said, "I need to go to work, but you need to know that God loves you and He has a plan for your life." I walked out the door to go to work, and it dawned on me — I didn't invite him to church. I turned and went back in and said, "Hey guys, I was just wondering if you'd want to go to church with me tomorrow?" My son's friend said, "Well that's funny. I just told your son that my grandma has been inviting me to church every week, and I keep telling her I'll go, and I just asked your son to go with me tomorrow." I smiled and said, "Well I think that's an awesome idea." Both of those boys were in church that very Sunday after God put that prayer in my heart. Oh, and one more thing. That boy got saved that Sunday and made Jesus the Lord of his life. He made a decision to live for the Lord, and that was over seven years ago. We are still friends on social media, and his story will always be one of the most fun miracles I've witnessed in a 24-hour period.

My prayer for those boys wasn't 12 hours long. It was during a specific time that I had set aside to meet with God. The Lord prompted me to pray for something specific and answered my prayer. I can't stress enough how important it is to set aside intentional time for God to speak to you and orchestrate miracles in your life. Prayer is the catalyst for life-changing miracles. God answers prayer. That's no small statement. When you truly grasp the power of prayer in your life, you'll never let another day go by without including it.

Mom's Prayers

I had a praying mama. One day we were talking about the power of a parent's prayer. We talked about the time I went out with a boy who had questionable character. I thought he was the greatest thing ever, but I was just getting to know him. Let's just say, it wasn't looking like he would be pastoring a church anytime soon.

Not too long ago, I asked my mom, "Isn't it strange how that guy just kind of disappeared from my life? I wonder what happened to him." Mom responded, "I know exactly what happened to him. I prayed him away." Praise God for praying parents! Mom knew this was not God's best plan for me. I smiled at Mom and thanked God for giving me a mom who would seek Him on my behalf. God intervened and rescued me because of my mama's prayers.

Parents, I can't encourage you enough to pray specifically for your children. So many times, God has put my sons on my heart, prompting me to stop and pray immediately for them. One of my boys remembers a time he was in a desperate situation and he asked me, "Mom were you praying for me last night?" And I was. Prayer activates angels and God-interventions.

It's a Date

Set an appointment every day to meet with God. This is a specific and guarded time to pray and ask God for wisdom and direction. I started with 30 minutes. It changed my life. In fact, I saw a change within 48 hours. Pray specifically, and watch your miracles unfold. That's powerful — and life-changing. And, if you think you're super busy, consider the words of Martin Luther, "I have so much to do that I shall spend the first three hours in prayer."

The first night I set aside this dedicated time to pray, I prayed for everyone I knew (and their pet) and the neighbors (and their pets). It seemed like I had been praying for three days. All I could think was that the sun should be coming up any moment. After what seemed to be at least four hours of praying, I looked at my phone, mostly because I thought the timer was broken. Nope, not broken. It had been 15 minutes, people. What the what? So, I decided to go back and start praying about specific situations in people's lives, challenges I knew my kids were going through, situations at work, my grandma's health, my cousin's children in college. I mean next-level prayer time. Wow, it was so good! The next thing I knew, my phone alarm went off because my 30 minutes was up.

I kind of wish you'd seen me when my alarm went off. You know when you're in deep thought (or prayer) and a fog horn goes off? It was pretty much like that. Not kidding. I nearly jumped out of my skin. Nevertheless, it was a great time of prayer. God was there. He heard my prayer, and I knew my life was about to get better. That's what's going to happen to you, too. Get ready!

Prayer is a commitment to say yes to God and goodbye to anything less than God's absolute best for you. Say goodbye to self and a resolute yes to the unknown. As you go before the

Lord, watch for and expect the supernatural — supernatural strength, supernatural vision, supernatural favor, supernatural appointments, and supernatural miracles. He is our rock, our salvation, and our protector. He will give you everything you need to navigate your season. Whether you're praying about a new job, healing, a kind marriage, or becoming newly single, quitting an addiction, or leaving your past behind, God is hearing you. He's fighting for you. Hope in Him will take you to your next season. Make your power move to pray and get ready for life-changing results. It was Oswald Chambers who wrote, "Prayer does not fit us for the greater work, prayer is the greater work."

ACTION STEP:

Create an appointment on your calendar that cannot be moved. Set reminders. Starting today, set aside 30 minutes of uninterrupted prayer time. "The effectual fervent prayer of a righteous man availeth much" (James 5:16, KJV). This verse implies that there are prayers that are not effectual and fervent. This time is intentional. Be effectual and fervent.

Effectual: Effective. Successful in producing a desired result.
Fervent: Having or displaying passionate intensity.

Day 2

THE WORD

*Fill your mind with God's Word
and you will have no room for Satan's lies.*

Ever since I was a little girl, I have loved to learn. I'm not sure I should admit to this, but in my spare time, in my preteen years, I loved to read the dictionary. I would study new words and try to use them in a sentence before the day ended. It was a little challenge I liked to add to my day. I didn't like homework, but I loved to learn what I wanted to learn. I followed my passion. I studied the things that made me happy or inspired me.

I had a dark-green, leather King James Bible that I would read nearly every night before bed. I memorized many Scriptures between the ages of 10 and 12 years old. Today, many of the verses I quote are the King James Version that I recall from my childhood. It's interesting how real God was to me at such a young age and the countless ways that He spoke to me through the King James Version, proof that God's Word truly is inspired. God speaks through His Word. I can still quote the verses I memorized at 10 years old. They never left my memory. Those verses have carried me through my whole life.

INSPIRATION

Inspiration has always been a big deal to me. During my teen years, I loved to sit at the piano and play for hours. I wrote songs to the Lord. I sang for hours. I may have heard the neighbor's dog howl while I sang, but whatever. I loved poems, too. I found an old tattered book of poems at my house that must have come from a great grandma. The hard cover was faded and worn around the edges and the pages were brownish. I didn't care. I loved the poems. They inspired me to write songs and poems of my own.

It's important that you know what inspires you. Don't get so busy paying the bills and doing "all the things" that you forget to make time for what inspires you. Inspiration comes from the Lord. God has given you the gift of inspiration and talents to accomplish beautiful things for His glory.

Inspiration will help you find your passion and calling. Maybe you love plants and gardening is your thing. Do you love to sew? Bake? Write? Sing? Encourage? Hunt? Fish? "Whatever you do, work at it with all your heart, as working for the Lord" (Colossians 3:23). Use your gifts and talents to bring joy to the Lord. Whatever reminds you that God has given you a beautiful life, do more of that.

Playing school was another favorite pastime of mine when I was young. I loved to play like I was a teacher. It was my favorite thing, I mean, besides hurting the neighborhood dogs' ears with my vocals. I love how God knows the desires of our hearts. I think He likes to surprise us and make some of those desires come to pass when we don't think He really even notices. Or, could it be that He put the desires inside of us in the first place, to accomplish His beautiful plan at just the right time in our lives? In the end, it's all His providential way of saying, "I see you. I hear you. I have a plan for you. I love you."

I'm so thankful I experienced the joy of homeschooling my sons, one of my favorite seasons of life. I enjoyed making a schedule that worked best for our family. The boys worked at a pace and learning style that caused them to flourish academically. I taught them until my oldest son was in third grade. I loved it so much. I cherished the time with them, and I loved watching them grow.

Then came the day we felt we should enroll the boys in private school. So, what's a homeschool mom to do? I began teaching at their school. God was so good to open doors for me to be close to my boys and do the thing I loved so much. I taught first and second grade. In fact, my youngest son was in my class. God gave me one more year to have him close to me. God loves to lavish us with gifts, and then we praise Him, and it becomes this beautiful circle of joy. We are surrounded by blessings every day to keep that circle going, if only we take the time to notice and give God praise.

I had so much fun teaching my first and second-graders. Such a sweet age group to teach. Truth be told, I may have watched too many episodes of "Little House on the Prairie" when I was young. Every morning I would walk into my classroom and my students would be sitting tall in their chairs, ready for class. In my happiest voice I would say, "Good morning class!" And every morning my class would respond in unison, "Good morning, Ms. Marla." I was the only teacher left in the school who still said the Lord's Prayer and the Pledge of Allegiance with my students. I couldn't be more thankful for the years God gave me to teach school. I loved my students dearly.

BEIGE TEETH

I had the cutest little first-graders on the planet. I loved the challenge of inspiring them to learn. I wanted school to be fun for them. I would help them get ready for a spelling test by walking around the room and asking them to find the items in our classroom that matched our spelling words. One day, our spelling word was "beige." I said, "Okay, class, look around the room and tell me if you see something beige?" Two students' hands shot up. I was so excited to see their little faces light up because they had the answer. I called on one eager young boy, "Okay, Timmy, I'm so happy you have an answer. What do you see that's beige in our room today?" Without hesitation, Timmy blurted out, "Your teeth, Ms. Marla!" All my little first-graders started nodding their heads as if to say, "Yay, Timmy! Good answer! He sure nailed that one!" I was standing in front of an honest room full of kids who didn't know how to do anything but call it like they see it. I always said, "You really need to have a lot of self-esteem to teach grade school children. They don't lie." Needless to say, I switched toothpaste and it's all good now.

OPPOSITE DAY

It was all good until the day we studied opposites. I thought for sure I'd be okay on this one. Then, the moment I asked the class, "Can anyone tell me the opposite of 'small'?" David shot his hand up. "Oh, pick me, Ms. Marla! I know! I know!" I said, "Okay, David, what's the opposite of 'small'?" David responded, "That's easy, Ms. Marla — YOU!" Then, silence in the room. "Oh, that's wonderful, David. Great answer. Good job, buddy." I mean, what do you say? "Good job, David! Hey, David, do you happen to know the number to a Weight Watchers club? I'll get right on that, little buddy." Those little boogers. You gotta love 'em.

NODDING TEACHER

There is one little story I'm hoping my second-graders don't remember as they look back on their elementary school days. (I think enough time has gone by that I won't get calls from parents.) It was the time I was reading to the class. They were all listening so intently with the cutest little faces you ever did see. They were all caught up in this awesome story I was reading to them, and the next thing I knew, every child in the classroom was uncontrollably laughing. I looked at the class and, trying to compose myself, said, "Um, what's so funny you guys?" One little sweetie from the back row shouted, "You fell asleep, Ms. Marla!" I looked around at all of the kids and they were rolling with laughter. I had to think fast. "Oh now, you crazy kids, what makes you say that?" They all started shouting, "Your eyes closed and you started saying silly words. You're so funny, Ms. Marla!" There was nowhere to go with that. I didn't have words. I didn't even know a person could do that. Apparently, you can actually read yourself a night-night story in the middle of the day until you fall asleep right in front of your entire second grade class. Oh, the memories. I'm so thankful God gave me the opportunity to teach. Those memories are some of my favorites of all time. I am incredibly inspired as I have watched God open doors and give me opportunities to do the things I love.

God wants to do the same for you! What are some things that bring you joy and inspire you to love this beautiful life? Ask God to open doors for you to experience more of that and then watch for those opportunities. God will surprise you with incredible seasons of miracles that you may have forgotten you prayed for. Don't miss it! Relish the season you're in, whether it's a season of solitude, a season of intense prayer, or a season of rejoicing – God is with you in this season.

REFLECTION

What does inspiration look like to you? I have a rule for myself. By the end of the day, I have to do something that inspires me. It can be a Jeep ride in the country, a long walk, or a latte at a bookstore. Sometimes my inspiration comes from quiet time, sitting next to my fireplace with a coffee. These moments of inspiration give me the gift of reflection, time to think about all of the miracles that have happened in my day and my life. These moments are critical for me to lead a hope-filled life. The same is true for you.

Take a moment and really think about what inspires your life. What makes you stop and smile and thank God for his blessings? If it's cooking, schedule the meals that you want to cook in the week. If it's reading to your kids, schedule it. It's important to do the things that bring you joy. These activities will remind you that God loves you and loves to bless you. I am a more passionate person because I make time in my day to be inspired and aspire to goals and dreams that God has given me. My day is more fulfilling when I allow time to reflect and recharge. I make sure I disconnect from work and social media. It makes a difference in my day, and it will in yours, too. Start with just a few minutes. I hope you find this to be one of your favorite new habits.

5-HOUR RULE

The 5-Hour Rule is a concept that involves setting aside five hours a week, or one hour each working day, dedicated to deliberate practice or learning. The key word is deliberate. My personal hour of learning involves at least 30 minutes of reading God's Word and 30 minutes of engaging in a book or video related to a goal I want to accomplish. Sometimes I do them together, or I do one at the beginning of the day and the other at the end of the day. Reading God's Word is the most important learning you can do in a day. If you only have time for one, let it be that one. Romans 15:4: "For everything that was written in the past was written to teach us, so that through the endurance taught in the Scriptures and the encouragement they provide we might have hope."

It's important to note that the 5-Hour Rule is not about consuming information. It is about intentional learning related to a goal or specific interest. It should be something that inspires you. With all of the options to learn right at your fingertips, you can listen to audio books or podcasts; read blogs, articles, and books about things you love or goals you want to accomplish. Ask God to direct your learning. Go to a local bookstore and spend an afternoon. Whatever interests you, study it next-level. There's so much to discover that will take your life to new, fun, and interesting places.

I love the challenge to learn one new thing every day that relates to a goal I have set for myself. I really enjoyed a 30-day project of creating what I wanted my future self to look like. I received daily emails that taught me how to set goals and attain them. I have also signed up to receive daily emails from different influencers that inspire me. I love the 5-Hour Rule that encourages me to make learning a priority. Learning is important, and I love that I've made it a rule for my life. It's become a non-negotiable rule to be my best self for everyone I love, and for me. The British philosopher, Alain de Botton, once said, "Anyone who isn't embarrassed of who they were last year probably isn't learning enough."[3]

God's Download

The most important source for hearing from our Almighty God is His Word. Your Creator has something to say to you. He wants to solve your problems. He wants to help you. He created you to need Him. "In the beginning was the Word, and the Word was with God, and the Word was God" (John 1:1). If you want to know what God thinks, how He works, what His will is, you must read His Word. That's where your answers are. If it's one verse or one chapter, read God's Word before your day ends. That is your weapon against the forces of darkness. Reading His Word guarantees you will hear from Him.

God gave us the gift of His Word to lead, direct, and protect us. Proverbs 30:5 tells us, "Every word of God is flawless; He is a shield to those who take refuge in Him." You will grow exponentially when you read God's Word. Every day you will get stronger. You will be hope-filled when you apply Psalm 119:114 to your life: "You are my refuge and my shield; I have put my hope in your word." You cannot fail when you hope in God's Word. Your hope is in the Almighty God. He is your power source. He is your refuge and shield. He will come through, and blessing will follow. "Keep this Book of the Law always on your lips; meditate on it day and night, so that you may be careful to do everything written in it. Then you will be prosperous and successful" (Josh 1:8).

As you commit to reading God's Word, you will hear from Him. Read a daily devotional specific to what you're going through (single parenting, a new job, moving to a new place) or whatever emotion you may be dealing with (sadness, an anxious heart, or fear). Download a reading plan on your phone and fill your heart with God's truth. You can read and/or listen to God's Word every day. Filling your mind with God's thoughts. As you meditate on God's Word, He will give you everything you need to move you to the next amazing season of your life.

God wants you to look forward to moments with Him. Combine inspiration and learning. Find a cozy place with a favorite coffee and prepare to hear from God and get supernatural wisdom from Him. Make your time special — not a have-to, but an inspirational time of get-to. Prepare your favorite latte or tea, play praise music, or enjoy the quiet, but make sure you create a time that you love. Make sure you have a committed amount of time and you don't feel rushed.

I like to split up my time with God. I read my Bible or devotional at a certain time, and my prayer time is at a different time. Be creative. Have fun. Light a candle. Sit in your favorite chair on your patio. Whatever you do, savor your time with God. This is your time to get real with Him. Share your deepest hurts and fears. Thank Him for your biggest wins, and seek His counsel for major decisions you need to make and goals you need to set.

We've got things to do, and we need God's supernatural vision and wisdom to get there. "Jesus answered, 'It is written: 'Man shall not live on bread alone, but on every word that comes from the mouth of God'" (Matt 4:4) This is priority. You can download your favorite Bible or devotional plan right now on your phone. It's fun to see all of the devotional options. I'll wait. The answers to our questions are in God's Word and found during the moments we are still enough to hear Him speak. I'm thankful for the black-and-white written words that steer our lives if we let them. In 2 Timothy 2:7 we read, "Reflect on what I am saying, for the Lord will give you insight into all this." Whatever creates an atmosphere of joy for you while you are learning, do that.

There was a time when my boys were young and I was working and could barely get everything done in a day — you know, trying to make sure they ate healthy and stayed alive. For real, all my boy-mom friends, you get it. Between skateboarding down treacherous hills, hunting with BB guns, paintballing — and God forbid I had a candle flame just sitting there not burning anything. You get the picture. I had less and less desire to make time for reading.

I did not love reading at all. It required a discipline of time that I was not willing to commit to. I had to pray, "God, please help me to love reading. I know growth is incredibly important, so I need Your help." He did it. He answered my prayer. Out of nowhere, I developed an insatiable desire to read. My friends would laugh because if you opened any book I was reading, you would see every line of the book highlighted. I had such a crazy passion for reading, only God could have instilled that in my heart. "If you remain in me and my words remain in you, ask whatever you wish, and it will be done for you" (John 15:7). I would encourage you to pray if you lack zeal for learning. God will help you like He helped me. A favorite saying of mine is, "If you are not willing to learn, no one can help you. If you are determined to learn, no one can stop you."

As you order your days, you will bring order to your life. Creating a time to hear from God, a time to learn, will inspire you to grow in your gifts and talents. This changes everything. "Learning is creation, not consumption. Knowledge is not something a learner absorbs, but something a learner creates" (George Couros).[4]

BREAKTHROUGH

An act or instance of removing or surpassing an obstruction or restriction; the overcoming of a stalemate.

As you spend time in prayer and reading God's Word, growth will happen. Finding books, videos, and podcasts from influencers who inspire you will take your life next-level. You are growing, and growth is progress. Progress leads to confidence. Confidence leads to single-minded vision. Once you are single-minded, you will have clarity and assurance that you're doing exactly what God has called you to do in this season of your life. A double-minded life is one of confusion and a lack of progress. "Such a person is double-minded and unstable in all they do" (James 1:8). Stop the confusion in your life. "For God is not the author of confusion but of peace" (1 Corinthians 14:33, ESV). God will calm the storms. That doesn't mean there won't be storms, but He will calm your heart to navigate them. Arrange your schedule and make it a priority to hear from God, and all the white noise will stop. God will give you clarity. He will give you peace. Keep your mind on Him, and listen for His direction. Isaiah 26:3 (ESV): "You keep him in perfect peace whose mind is stayed on you, because he trusts in you." A peace-filled life is a beautiful thing and a testimony to your friends and family.

There are so many opportunities to grow stronger. We want to grow in our walk with God, and become mentally and physically strong and healthy. This magnificent, wonderful world is full of peak experiences we have yet to enjoy. Ask God to help you and He will lead you. As you choose good habits over bad ones, every area of your life will get brighter. You will stack good habits and they will compound. You will easily implement them into your day and they will become a part of your life. Grow in your commitment to study God's Word, grow in your job, grow in your healthy eating habits, take your workouts to a new level. Start preparing your mind to think bigger. Avoid doing what you've always done lest you get what you've always gotten. "I press on toward the goal to win the prize for which God has called me heavenward in Christ Jesus." (Philippians 3:14) As you press on, break-through is the prize, hope is on the horizon!

You are either moving forward or losing ground. There is no status quo, according to Pierce Marrs.[5] Your family and others need you. Your growth will inspire people on their paths. During seasons of praying and waiting on God for miracles, be busy growing. This is faith in action.

God sees you in this season. He hears every prayer. He sees the bigger picture. Run after Him diligently. Trust His timing. "But those who hope in the Lord, will renew their strength. They will soar on wings like eagles; they will run and not grow weary; they will walk and not be faint" (Isa. 40:31). You have a job to do while you wait – GROW.

Make your next power move today by planning your time of inspiration and growth. What will you do first? Prayer, a devotion, and a Bible app? Prayer, a devotion, and a new book? Put your plan in place and start as soon as possible. It was during my time with the Lord that I was prompted to write this book. That only happened because of my commitment to spend time with Him. He spoke to my heart. I pray that for you. I pray that you commit this season to growth and hearing from God regarding your next power moves.

As you implement 30 minutes of solid prayer and one hour of time to learn from God's Word and some great influencers, you will see immediate change. The change will start on the inside, which will lead to change on the outside. These are power moves. Power moves are action steps. An action step may include the elimination of a distraction in your life. If there is something distracting you from running after God every day, remove it immediately. Again, we are making bold moves to make major life changes in 15 days. There is no time to play with distractions that keep you from getting close to God.

God has equipped you with everything you need to accomplish what He has put in your heart. Take action and build your life. Creating your future starts with making power moves today.

Action Step:

Write down the power moves you are going to implement. Talk about it. Tell a friend. Solidify your plan. Prepare for big results that come from big power moves. This move might be to add something to your agenda, or it may require removing something (a distraction).

Day 3

ONE PERCENT WEEKLY

The greatest legacy one can pass on to one's
children and grandchildren is not money...
but rather a legacy of character and faith.
—Billy Graham

We have 168 hours in a week. A typical church service is usually two hours of my week. That is exactly one percent of the week to spend in the house of God (unless you live in Africa, where a service can last six to eight hours; they have next-level church). This is a time to meet with other believers and give God the glory for more blessings than I could ever list in a single book like this. It's a specific time to seek God for all that is happening in our lives individually and corporately in the exact same moment in time. We already know God loves when two or more pray, and He wants us to fellowship with other believers. This isn't optional; we've got to get to church!

True statement: the church has been my refuge my whole life long. The church is the one place God loves more than all other places. The Bible says He is "building His church." It is the place I go to hear God's Word and get strong for my battles. I'm reminded that He will supply all of my needs and He loves me; my faith increases with every service. Romans 10:17 tells us that "faith comes from hearing the message." Listening to the Word of God at His house will increase your faith. That is powerful. Faith will keep you strong. Faith will give you hope in a desperate situation. No matter the season of my life, when I have stayed close to God, His Word, and His church, He has carried me through every valley. I know that my recovery time from past hurts has happened exponentially faster because of my decision to stay faithful to the house of God. I become stronger as I lean in to all that God is doing in His church. God inhabits the praises of His people. And, remember Matthew 18:20? "For where two or three gather in my name, there am I with them." Stay close to other believers. The church is your refuge. It is a non-negotiable in a believer's life and the place I run to for wisdom, encouragement, and strength. I know God will meet me there, just like He will meet you there.

It was my first Sunday to attend church after the divorce from my boys' father. I was beyond distraught. I felt like such a failure. I had disappointed God and felt it was completely futile to believe that God still had a plan for me. As I was walking to my seat, all I could think was the message would probably be all about the failure of divorce. I was preparing myself to accept that God was so displeased with my life, how could He ever really love a mess like me? How could I expect anything good for my life, ever?

I sat down and listened as my pastor began to talk about God's great love. He began to cry and said, "God loves you. You could never run too far from His love. You need to know how much He loves you." I could feel the tears running down my cheeks. That's the last thing I expected. I couldn't believe what I was hearing. How was it even possible that the message could be about how much God loves me? I was completely overwhelmed by God's love that day. I began to pray and just thank Him for loving me. I spent the next few moments trying to grasp that concept and believe it. My prayer for you is that God will show you how much He loves you. I pray that you make time for church, where you will be reminded that God never leaves you or forsakes you, even in your darkest moments. He's still there. No matter what season you are in, He loves you deeply. He still has a plan, and it's a good one.

House of Hope

Church is one of the most beautiful gifts from God. You will find encouragement, friendship, and hope. Church is a good place to make lifelong friends and find people you want influencing your life and the lives of your children. Don't miss out on one of the most valuable resources from God just because someone in the church hurt you. We've all been there. People hurt us at work and in our families sometimes, too. Hurt is just part of this imperfect journey. Don't let the enemy steal one more Sunday, one more opportunity to live your best life. Gathering with other believers who love God and are committed to His church must be a top priority.

If you want the absolute best church experience of your life, go to church to give not to get. When you walk in the doors, look for someone to hug, someone to encourage, someone to smile at, and you will feel God's presence every single time. If you walk in the doors waiting to see who will talk to you, who will hug you, who will encourage you, the outcome of your experience most likely will disappoint. Church is a place to pour into others. Proverbs 11:25 (ESV): "Whoever brings blessing will be enriched, and one who waters will himself be watered." Drive up to the parking lot looking for people to wave to, someone to give a parking space to, someone to motion to go ahead of you in the car line. You will never lose when you love people in God's house. Church is the place people come for healing. It's the one place they go for hope. God will use you to be salve to a hurting soul, to speak life to a hopeless heart, to encourage a broken spirit. One of the ways God shows his love to people is through other people. God meets us at church. He loves His church, and we love the things God loves.

THE FOOD PANTRY

There was a time when the boys and I were running low on food. I was starting my new job and had not gotten paid yet. I wasn't sure what I was going to do. My pastor's wife asked if I needed help. I didn't know what to say. She made a call, and the next thing I knew, the church family gathered groceries from the food pantry for me and brought them to my car. I watched as God provided a miracle for me and the boys through our church family.

I couldn't wait to go home and show the boys what God had done for us. I took all of the groceries out of the car and lined them all across the kitchen counter. I called the boys in and showed them. "Look boys! God is providing everything we need." I think the boys saw pop-tarts and knew God was a God of miracles!

DINNER

I'm not sure the boys believed that we really needed store-bought food. I can explain. My boys spent most of their childhood trying to convince me that we could live on everything they hunted and caught in the yard or the woods behind the house. One night they were on a serious mission. My instructions from them were, "Prepare the sides, Mom. We got the meat. We'll be back soon." I was scared. I don't remember what sides I made, nor do I know what sides you prepare for rabbit, squirrel and cute little birds. Yeah, the next time you girl-mommies tell me how rough it is, I'm bringing pictures over to show you a day with sons and their "kill" in your kitchen.

One impactful moment for me was the day I was able to replenish the groceries I had been given from the food pantry at church. I had started receiving paychecks, and it was my turn to bless another single mom. I'm thankful God gave me the opportunity to give back. I was thankful to be blessed and then to be a blessing to another family in their time of need. The boys and I never needed financial help again. All of our needs were met in that season because God provided everything we needed. God will take care of you every time. Stay close to His house.

Finances

I would be remiss if I didn't tell you about God's amazing financial provision over the years as I have tithed to His house. "'Bring the whole tithe into the storehouse, that there may be food in my house. Test me in this,' says the LORD Almighty, 'and see if I will not throw open the floodgates of heaven and pour out so much blessing that there will not be room enough to store it'" (Mal 3:10). This is the one Scripture in the Bible where God says, "test me and see."

It was a Wednesday night, and they were receiving the offering at church. I was newly single with two sons. I was still getting my bearings and trying to find a job that would allow me to be home with the boys when they came home from school. Money was scarce, but I looked in my purse and I had a $5 bill. I remember praying, "Lord, this is all I have to my name and I don't even have a job yet. I know You can meet all of my needs. I'm giving this offering and looking forward to all the ways You will provide. In the name of Jesus, Amen."

On that Friday (two days later), I was in a resale shop thinking I would need work clothes. As I was looking through the clothes, the owner greeted me. I said, "Hello," and kept looking at the clothes. Out of nowhere, she said, "By any chance, would you be interested in a job?" My mouth dropped. I said, "Oh my goodness, yes! My sons are in school. What hours would you need me?" She said, "Well, I only need part time, so you could get off at 3 p.m." I almost started to cry. Guess who started the following Monday? Only God could have provided that job in that way.

I knew that a part-time job would not pay all of the bills, so I began to wonder what my next plan would be. I went to church on Sunday morning. Following that service, I was walking through a hallway and I heard someone call my name. I turned and saw a man standing there. He said, "My name is Josh. I know you don't know me, but we have a mutual friend who told me you might be looking for a job. I am needing a part-time assistant and was wondering if you'd be interested?" I could not believe what I was hearing. I couldn't say YES fast enough and started two weeks later.

Only God. I gave $5 on Wednesday, and God gave me two part-time jobs, allowing me to be home for my sons by Sunday. I didn't even apply for either job. Both bosses came to me and offered me the jobs. I didn't even know either of them. When we do our part, God will chase us down with blessings — specific blessings that meet all of our needs.

ANOTHER FUN MIRACLE

Let's talk about the time I miscalculated my tithe. I wrote a check on Sunday morning and placed it in the offering, and after the offering bucket had passed, I realized I had written the check for the wrong amount. Let's just say it was about $250 more than what I meant to write, and thus $250 more than what I had in my bank account. I literally sat in my seat and repeated, "Oh dear Lord Jesus, I know I could chase down the usher, but I don't believe that's the answer. Besides, You know, Lord, I'd probably fall down a flight of steps in these heels. I'm asking You for a miracle. Those funds are not in my account. Oh Lord, I know nothing is too hard for You. You are the God of miracles and I could really use one today. I know that You can provide the funds to cover that miscalculation. I pray for a miracle in the name of Jesus."

Four days later, I was home on Thursday night and my doorbell rang. I went to the door and there on my porch stood a couple who had a son who was friends with my son. I didn't know them all that well, but I knew they were Christians and were really kind. I opened the door, and the wife said, "Hi. We don't want this to seem crazy, but God told us to bring you a check tonight. We felt led to bring it to you and we pray that it is a blessing to you." They handed me the check. I turned it over and it was in the amount of $500, exactly double the amount I had miscalculated and gave on Sunday. Tears came to my eyes. Only God.

I'm so thankful my mom taught me to always tithe – first. Since my very first paycheck, I have always tithed, and I cannot remember a time when I have gone without one thing I needed. God has always provided for me. The fact is, God doesn't need our money. He needs us to obey Him so He can bless us like crazy. He loves to do that. He asks us to be cheerful givers. "Each one must give as he has decided in his heart, not reluctantly or under compulsion, for God loves a cheerful giver" (2 Corinthians 9:7, ESV). If you have never tithed, you have to believe me when I tell you how fun it is to watch God bless your finances. Honestly, it's amazing watching God outdo anything we think we are sacrificing. It's not a sacrifice at all when you get way more in return. It's all about trust — trusting God will do His part. Make sure you journal this journey, because it will be fun to look back and read.

Always smile when you write your check or see the debit from your bank account. You know that as you walk in obedience blessing is heading your way. Choose joy. What an incredible opportunity to be a part of building God's house by contributing finances. You can't help but have joy when you realize a financial miracle is on the way when you tithe. A cheerful heart is easy when you know God is about to show up in your situation.

Making a Difference

Volunteering is one of the most beautiful ways to be God's hand extended to the people on your path. As you give of your time to help others, on the other side of your generosity, God actually blesses you. You cannot outgive God, not with your finances, nor your time.

Walking in obedience with a heart to serve the Lord at church will change your life. You are now a part of the body of Christ. Love these verses in 1 Corinthians 12:12-27:

> [12] Just as a body, though one, has many parts, but all its many parts form one body, so it is with Christ. [13] For we were all baptized by one Spirit so as to form one body—whether Jews or Gentiles, slave or free—and we were all given the one Spirit to drink. [14] Even so the body is not made up of one part but of many. [15] Now if the foot should say, "Because I am not a hand, I do not belong to the body," it would not for that reason stop being part of the body. [16] And if the ear should say, "Because I am not an eye, I do not belong to the body," it would not for that reason stop being part of the body. [17] If the whole body

were an eye, where would the sense of hearing be? If the whole body were an ear, where would the sense of smell be? [18] But in fact God has placed the parts in the body, every one of them, just as he wanted them to be. [19] If they were all one part, where would the body be? [20] As it is, there are many parts, but one body. [21] The eye cannot say to the hand, "I don't need you!" And the head cannot say to the feet, "I don't need you!" [22] On the contrary, those parts of the body that seem to be weaker are indispensable, [23] and the parts that we think are less honorable we treat with special honor. And the parts that are unpresentable are treated with special modesty, [24] while our presentable parts need no special treatment. But God has put the body together, giving greater honor to the parts that lacked it, [25] so that there should be no division in the body, but that its parts should have equal concern for each other. [26] If one part suffers, every part suffers with it; if one part is honored, every part rejoices with it. [27] Now you are the body of Christ, and each one of you is a part of it.

Be a Team Player

Training our children to be team players, team players for Jesus, that's what matters. Parents sometimes talk about the value of sports in a child's life. I've heard some parents say that sports create a sense of community, a sense of teamwork, a sense of commitment and loyalty. Have you ever noticed, all of that is also what makes a church thrive? Training children to be team players at the house of God, now you're building more than a sports team, you're building a legacy.

My mom's commitment to choir was like that of a quarterback playing for the best team in the NFL. She didn't miss practice. She didn't miss a service. She was committed. She sang in the choir as unto the Lord, with excellence. She didn't think she was the best on the team, but I'm not kidding; she was committed like they couldn't win if she wasn't there to do her part. That's commitment. She never sang one solo. Not one. She never had a leading part, but she knew she was part of something bigger than a four-minute song. She was doing her part in the body of Christ.

Mom had a full-time job and still didn't miss a weekday practice. She drove to the church when she had worked a long day and was tired. She smiled and gave 100 percent when she got there. We lived pretty far away from the church. Most people in choir knew we didn't live close, but they knew

Sheila would be there. The drive didn't matter to her. She was on a mission for Jesus. The most important mission you could ever commit to, building God's house.

Mom was training me every time we got in the car and headed to church. She showed me what true commitment to God's house looked like. This commitment yielded rewards that would follow me for a lifetime. I experienced the joy of being part of a team making an eternal difference. I discovered that in volunteering was true joy — without a paycheck. She taught me the value of a single person's role and responsibility as part of the body of Christ.

The interesting thing is, my mom wasn't raised in a family that went to church every week. She made a commitment to the Lord at a young age and had to find rides to church. Her commitment didn't come from a long history of preachers in the family. She just loved God and wanted to serve Him excellently. And that, she did.

INVITES

Inviting people to church is the most important work we can do. You may meet people who are overwhelmed with a heavy load. You may feel underqualified to help them. None of us are qualified, and that is why we invite people to church where God can meet their needs. We don't have the answers, but we can take them to the One who does. God never intended for us to carry heavy burdens. He says, "Come to me, all you who are weary and burdened and I will give you rest" (Matthew 11:28). We invite people to church so we can take them to the healer of all brokenness, the redeemer of our pasts, the comforter of our souls.

PRAY

Ask God to lead you to the place He would want you to volunteer at your church. Make a commitment to be all-in for six months or a year. Give your absolute best and watch God reward your efforts in ways you never would have imagined. To be part of the body of Christ, we need to engage and help build the church. God will show you someone who may need to hear a kind word; someone who will choose to hope again after seeing the love of God in your countenance. God can show you a visitor who needs assurance that God loves them, a young person who needs to know that God is hearing them. Someone may need your joy as they fight through an incredibly tough battle. You may be the reason someone chooses not to give up. Maybe you will meet someone going to church for the first time after experiencing a great loss. God may show His love through you and give an addict a reason to believe that God still loves them and wants to help them. You could be part of an incredible miracle as you volunteer at God's house.

Make bold power moves toward hope today. Implement non-negotiables in your life. Build your relationship with God, pray, and read His written Word. Be in His presence at church. Tithe and watch God meet your needs. Allow God to reveal new things to you and be prepared for supernatural favor in your endeavors. God will open doors that can only open through Him. Preferential treatment and kindness, raises and blessings, are what come with a life consecrated in God. There will be trials, but have no fear. God gave us a word to stand on. "In this world you will have trouble. But take heart! I have overcome the world" (John 16:33).

God's desire is for you to have hope and joy. Prepare for days to celebrate. You will see God do what only He can do. No matter what your circumstances look like at this moment, God is going to give you joy and peace that passes all understanding. He's going to give you wisdom and provide all that you need to take you where you need to go. Ephesians 3:20 (NLT): "Now all glory to God, who is able, through His mighty power at work within us, to accomplish infinitely more than we might ask or think."

The most powerful move you can make in your life is to be totally committed to God. It is no accident that I wrote this book right after I implemented a seriously committed plan to seek the Lord. He told me what to write about. He told me what to title it. He gave me the words. There are miracles in your life that will occur on the other side of your commitment to spend time with God. I'm so excited for you just thinking about it!

ACTION STEP:

Attend church this week. Make it a new priority every week of your life. Dive in, contribute to God's house, volunteer, and watch God bless your efforts, your family, and your life.

Day 9

WRITE YOUR OWN STORY

This is your beautiful story. Write it any way you'd like.

I once heard it said that if you really want to know people, listen to their stories. Better yet, listen to how they tell their stories. Are they typically the victim? Was everything done to them? Every story of our lives could go that way, right? The question is, does that perspective serve us? Does that story strengthen and empower our futures? Not even a little bit.

Our growth, strength, and joy come when we remove ourselves as the victim from every single story. Does that mean it was all fair or right? No. Remember the saying, "That which does not kill you will only make you stronger." It's true. If you choose, you can be stronger because of your life experiences, every single one of them, even the ones that hurt. You cannot change history, but you can change the feelings you have about your history. You can ask God to start healing your heart. He will.

You may have a story that you've been replaying in your mind for years. Is it stealing your joy? It's time to rewrite that story. Ask God to help you reframe it. You can actually take a sad story and turn it into an empowering story if you emphasize the right parts of it. Tell your story in such a way that you can smile when you share it. I know it's a tall order, but I also know that the minute you do this, you're finally free.

IT HAPPENED *FOR* ME

One of the most powerful phrases to remember is, "Everything in my life didn't happen *to* me, it happened *for* me."[6] We all have things in our lives that didn't go as planned. Have you allowed that disappointment to control your happiness, your hope for the future? Maybe you were treated unfairly, maybe even abused. Something happened to you and it was beyond your control. We've all been there. One particular event in my life hurt me more than all others. There was nothing I could do to change what happened, and wow, did it ever hurt. I made up my mind to apply this perspective, "it happened for me, not to me," and everything changed. I would literally say it out loud every time I thought about it until I finally believed it.

I had to accept that I could not go back and change the past. What I could do is *build* my future. Every time I look back, I go that way – backwards. When I look forward, I have hope and see a world full of opportunity. You know there is no perfect life. Not one. No one avoids all pain and disappointment. The question is, how will you navigate it? Maybe at one time you set goals and had dreams for your life that didn't turn out as you imagined. It's time to set new goals and dreams, starting right where you are, at this moment in time. What if your amazing future is lining up for you starting with your story right now, as in this very moment that you are reading this book? THIS is your new beginning. Now, you have a starting point, something to build on. God gave us a promise in Psalm 71:20, "Though you have made me see troubles, many and bitter, you will restore my life again; from the depths of the earth, you will again bring me up."

As you follow God, sometimes you get sweet surprises like, "Oh my word! That turned out way better than I could have ever planned!" Other times, you shake your head in disbelief, "I can't believe it went that way." The healthiest perspective is to accept both. "I don't see the big picture Lord. Only You do. Therefore, I will trust." When I truly believe that, peace follows every time. It took a few days of rehearsing this perspective, "I am not a victim. Those things happened for me, not to me." The next thing I did was reach out to a person who hurt me and healing took place. A relationship was restored. If you had told me that could ever happen, I'm not sure I would have believed it.

YOUR POWER, YOUR CHOICE

I remember someone asking me about my divorce. Out of nowhere, I replied, "Oh, yes, that was a difficult season, but God is so good and we are on the other side of it now." I used to feel obligated to talk about every detail of my life, which did not serve me well. There was no time to explain the devastation of divorce after 20 years of growing up together. I couldn't explain it to every person who asked, so, I rewrote my story of trauma in my head and turned it into a story that didn't devastate my soul to talk about.

A couple of years ago, someone I had grown close to over the years said one of the kindest things to me. "I can't help but notice that when you talk about your past, you never say one ugly word about your ex-husband. Not one." I can't tell you the joy that filled my heart. I felt like it was confirmation that healing had taken place in my heart, and I was so thankful. God did that. In that moment, all I could think was, "Thank you, God. I know that was You."

Imagine you are Superman, and the really bad stories of your past are your kryptonite. What if every negative story (kryptonite) where you were the victim, was making you weaker by the day and you were losing all of your power? But what if all you had to do was rewrite those stories and you would start regaining your strength, your powers? What if you rewrote those stories, and all of a sudden, bullets ricocheted off of you and you started flying again, and this time, you flew higher than ever? That's the power of rewriting your past and making it a story that works *for* you, not *against* you. You come out stronger.

We all have good and not-so-good memories of our pasts. I have been through some rough experiences that not many people have been through, but I do not want that to be the story of my life. I have a choice. I choose to focus on the wonderful things in my past, because there were those, too. It doesn't mean it was all perfect. It means I get to remember the best things. I have too many wonderful days ahead of me to be angry, hurt, or bitter because of a few not-so-great things in my past. I'm too excited about the incredible opportunities ahead. You get to make that same choice. Focus on what you want more of. Awesome opportunities are on the way for you!

Dan Sullivan said, "Always make your future bigger than your past."[7] Your true identity comes from your view of your future, not your past. You have the power to choose to write your past into a healthy story that will give you peace and the ability to look back without anger. If you're able to heal a relationship in the process, that's a bonus.

No one gets to tell you how damaging or dysfunctional your past was. Only you get to make that decision. This principle is called "agency." In social science, agency is defined as the capacity of individuals to act independently and make their own free choices.[8] You have agency, the power to choose whether you will be the victim or the victor in your story.

Remember, this is your story. Write it the way you want. You get to choose how long it takes to recover from painful events. And by recover, I am referring to how long it takes for you to be able to frame your story in a way that doesn't devastate you or make you angry. How much time does healing take? There's no rule or formula for that. The timeframe for your healing and recovery is up to you. There is no right or wrong answer. You choose.

Dr. Benjamin Hardy says, "Trauma is a dysfunctional framing of your experience."[9] Past trauma hurts. Trauma requires healing. You are steering the ship. If you want to steer toward healing, you must change the meaning you give your past experiences. Remove any ugly descriptions of people involved, and instead, talk about the growth that happened inside of you. Talk about how you navigated through it — and now look at you. Remove anything that puts you in the victim seat. Instead, make yourself the hero in your story. You can speak about your past with a supernatural peace. No more kryptonite! God will help you.

I have many friends who have spent years dissecting their pasts with licensed or certified experts. After years of counsel, and a reinforcement of their pain and damage that was done, they were told why they are "this way" or "that way." Recent research is proving that individuals have a choice in how they view their pasts. This is why there is also evidence that when people resolve that their pasts happened for them and not to them, they experience healing and recovery at an exponentially higher rate.

Finish Strong

Your current behavior consists of choices you are making today. A painful and less-than-perfect past does not cause you to make bad decisions in your present. Past events may influence your thought process and how you make decisions, but they don't determine your choices today. You get to choose. Don't let anyone take that away from you. Use your past to help you make better decisions today. Frame your story to set yourself up to win and finish strong.

I'm reminded of a story of two brothers who were raised by an alcoholic father. One brother grew up and became an alcoholic. When asked why, he replied, "My father was an alcoholic." The other brother grew up and wouldn't touch alcohol. When asked why, he replied, "My father was an alcoholic." Is your story of your past weakening or strengthening your future? Use your past to remind you of the miracle your life is today. Your experience can cause you to have greater empathy for others who have gone through similar pain. Your story can give others hope for a brighter future. Your past is not your life anymore. Your story can actually serve you. Get ready for a powerful life. Be brave. Run your race like a 3 year old with new light-up tennis shoes!

Your future is bright. You are growing and becoming; that is the path you are on. Every day is a beautiful opportunity to live life better than the day before. Once you have a relationship with Jesus, you become "...a new creature; the old has passed away; behold, the new has come" (2 Cor. 5:17, ESV). Stand on God's Word. Stand on His promises. We all have a past. We have all made mistakes, as Romans 3:23 (ESV) tells us, "For all have sinned and fall short of the glory of God." Our mission now is to grow into the person we want to be. Hope says we can be anyone or anything we want to be. Your past, no matter what it looked like, can actually be the catalyst to take you to new heights in your life. Here's the deal: no one can make the decision for you. Only you can choose healing and new heights. Only you have the power to turn your story into a wonderful story of victory and triumph. The sooner you do that, the faster you'll meet new goals and enjoy the future you have prayed for.

Marian's Story

We all need a Marian in our lives. I met Marian at a gym 9 or 10 years ago. She had lovely white hair and leaned forward when she walked. She was the cutest 85-year-old ever. I noticed she was walking on the track by herself, so I asked if I could join her. We walked and talked, and I loved her stories. Over the next few months, we would meet pretty regularly and catch up on life. I remember when her husband passed away. She remembers when I would ask for parenting advice. One day, we just started doing life together.

After a few years of walking together, she invited me to her house for tea. We had a lovely visit. Then, the day came when she could no longer go to the gym. She was probably 90 at that time. I have made it a point to go visit her at her home regularly over the last several years. Sometimes, I take Chinese food, and we sit at her kitchen table and share stories about life. I love to hear her stories from the '40s, '50s, and so on. She makes me laugh, and I love to make her laugh. She makes choices every day to thrive. She loves to read. But if you really want to get her fired up, talk about politics. Her friendship is a gift to me.

On a wall in her hallway hangs a large photo of her in her 20s. She's so beautiful. She told me the photo was taken about the time she was in modeling school. Her smooth skin, perfectly coifed hair, big blue eyes, and sweet smile were stunning. I look at that photo and have such respect for the life she has lived, every year she's owned, every child she's raised, every city she's lived in, every job she's had, every story of overcoming.

I have always felt that Marian (now 95 years young) was a gift from God. She talks about the good things in life. She tells stories about hard times and then says, "God was with me through it all." Sometimes she'll talk about a husband who left her, and then a husband who died of cancer, and then the next husband who died from illness. She's been through so much, but she always includes something good about every season of her life. She had three children and has outlived all of them but one son. Marian is a beautiful reminder that whatever you've been through, you made it through.

One day, Marian invited me over and she had another friend at her house. The friend was about her age and began to share stories of years gone by. Oh dear. Her stories were horrible. What was interesting is that some of her stories actually ended better than Marian's or mine, but you couldn't tell her that. She wanted to talk about the misery, the pain, and the injustice. I witnessed two women, very close in age, who had framed their stories completely differently. I listened to these ladies and thought, "One day I will be that age. What stories will I tell?" I pray that I can tell them like Marian tells them, remembering that God was there through it all. She reminds me that life is constantly changing, but God does not change. The way things are today will not always be. We are not promised tomorrow. We only have this moment. Praise God for this moment and don't bother worrying about tomorrow, that's just a waste of precious time.

I hope you can find a friend like Marian to encourage and be encouraged by. We all have a choice to make. We can choose Marian's story, and live it well and tell it well, or choose her friend's discouraging story. Choose your thoughts and words carefully. Frame your stories in a way that encourages the people around you and YOU. We have places to go, people to love, and dreams to fulfill. We need to tell a better story of our past so that we can experience a bigger and brighter future.

FRAMING YOUR CHILDHOOD

Your opportunities, growth, and mental health depend on the story you've written about your past. I have a friend whose childhood looked quite similar to mine. Her father worked long hours, just like mine. However, her father came home most nights, while my father traveled and I didn't see him as often. One day, she began telling me that she had to work through forgiving her father for not being there for her. I just listened in shock. Her father had been home much more than mine. It was interesting how she had framed her story.

If you listen to my stories about my father, you'd think I had the perfect family with a father who came home every evening at 5 p.m. to join us for dinner at 5:30. That wasn't my life at all. My dad was out of town three to five days every week. As I was growing up, I knew he worked hard. I remember crying myself to sleep so many nights because I missed him. I remember crying on the phone when he'd call because I wished he would come home. I don't talk about that part. At an early age I decided to speak about the two or three days that I got to spend time with my Daddy. The days he took me fishing, the summers at the lake, him coaching my softball team on the weekends, that's my story and I'm stickin' to it. (Okie talk) I have so many wonderful stories. No one would really know that I didn't see him most of the week, most of my childhood. I wrote a story that made me feel happy and love my life with my dad.

Everyone has a story. Choose one that makes you thankful for your journey. Choose the part of your story that makes your heart peaceful and loving. Focus on the highlights of your childhood that make you smile. They are there, but you have to choose them.

The Bible says your "tongue has the power of life and death" (Prov. 18:21). Words matter. This includes the words about your present and your future, but also the words describing your past. You are a stronger person today because of every single thing you've been through until now. The words you choose will empower you or victimize you. "Kind words are like honey, sweet to the soul and healthy for the body" (Prov. 16:24, NLT). You can actually speak kind words over yourself and your past and have a healthier body.

Speak life. Use life-giving words to describe your past. This may mean taking some time to talk to the Lord and ask for His help. You may need to spend time alone and decide what your new story will be. Maybe you need to journal it. Keep writing it until it's like a salve over your heart. You may even find that your new story about your past will bring a smile to your face. As you take hold of this beautiful reframing of your past, you will experience a new peace. Own your past, and you will own your future.

Pass It On

As parents, we have the opportunity and responsibility to train our children to choose their words carefully and to help them write their own stories. While they are young, we can show them how to frame the events of their days, their lives, in ways that leave no room for them to be victims.

My parents were amazing examples of training my sister and me to choose how we framed our experiences. I was in sixth grade and came home from school one day devastated because a girl at school didn't like me. My wonderful mother, strong and wise, reframed that story for me. She looked at me and said, "Well honey, if someone doesn't like you, it's just because they don't know you. If they knew you, they would love you." She strengthened me for the rest of my life. Those words would echo in my mind, always. Mom taught me to be compassionate toward people who weren't kind to me. After all, they just didn't know me.

My mom always trained and empowered me to choose healthy thoughts about a situation. She showed me, by example, where to turn for help. She gave God all the glory for her strength and wisdom. As a young teen, I would come home from school, walk in the front door and see Mom's Bible open on the coffee table, her pen next to it, and many verses underlined. There was never a doubt that my mom was praying and seeking God on behalf of our family.

My father often quoted Proverbs 23:7 (KJV), "As a man thinketh in his heart, so is he." It all starts with your thoughts. He would encourage my sister and me to think strong, positive thoughts about ourselves and our situations. He wanted us to believe we were smart, kind, and special. One time, I came home from school with a "C" in Spanish. Dad came to me and said, "What's this?" I looked up at him and I said, "Dad it's a 'C'. That means average." Without skipping a beat, he looked right at me and said, "Exactly, and you're not average." My parents were amazing at keeping the bar high and encouraging us to rise to it. They didn't lower the bar to accommodate bad behavior or poor choices.

Dad was also a big fan of Zig Ziglar. I'm the product of a father who spoke life over his family. He would encourage me to look for the good in everyone and focus on those things. He would say, "If you look for everything someone does wrong, that's what you'll find. Look for the things they're doing right." Apply this thought to your past. There were good times. There were painful times. There were times of growth. There were times that strengthened you. Look for the good that came from your past and write your new story.

All day, every day, we are writing stories in our minds — stories about our day, or the way people treat us at work, in our home, in our extended family. We even write stories about people we don't know, such as servers and other drivers.

I always have the same story when I drive behind someone going below the speed limit, or not signaling, or cutting me off in traffic. I say, "I bet that's an older person, probably like my grandma. They probably didn't even see me, or maybe they don't feel good today." That's my story. When someone makes a mistake driving, what story are you telling yourself? Question that story, and question your response to the story. Is that what really happened? Driving in traffic is one of the best opportunities to master the art of creating a beneficial story in your mind. Do you leave room for the other people involved to possibly feel differently than the meanings you may attach to their actions? How positive and gracious is your story about the actions of others? When you can master the story you are telling yourself about other people's driving, you will be on the road to a happy heart (and maybe less shouting and road rage). Driving is also the perfect opportunity to teach our children to choose a story that brings peace when we can't explain other people's actions.

SOMETIMES LIFE JUST ISN'T FAIR

We tell ourselves stories to navigate the challenges of our lives. Happy and sad are both part of the journey. We would all love a life of 24/7 joy but that isn't how it works. Sadness in life is part of it, and normal. Ecclesiastes 3:4: "There is a time to weep and a time to laugh." You will cry, you will laugh. Variety is part of the beauty of this life. When you're sad, God says that's okay. It doesn't necessarily mean you're depressed or need a permanent diagnosis. It doesn't always mean you have anxiety and should be labeled for the rest of your days. It means you have a broken heart. Allow yourself to process painful things in your life, but process it with God and people who love you. Seek God, start praising Him for your comeback, attend church every time the doors are open, and see what happens with your perspective on life. Give God the opportunity to heal your heart. God will help you and that can look like many different things. He will never turn you away when you ask Him for help. You will walk through seasons. Make the decision to navigate each season with God's help. Choose healing as God fights your battles. Be strong and courageous. Remember that God is on your side and He is your protector.

Start today

Write a kind story about your life. Use words like grace, mercy, and forgiveness, three of the most beautiful words. Write a story that will keep your heart soft. The softer your heart, the more radiant your countenance. The more grateful you are for your past, the healthier your future.

Ask God to heal your heart today. No matter who or what was part of your pain, make a decision today not to let hurtful thoughts steal one more minute of your life. Ask God to help. He will. He will help you hope again. It's up to you to choose encouraging thoughts and do the work to move toward healing. You have a choice to dwell on the sad or "take every thought captive" (2 Cor. 10:5) and start writing your new story. It's time to heal. If you have children, the sooner the better. It's okay if you need a little time. If you are spending time with God every day, He will guide you.

Walk through pain; don't park there. Keep walking. Choose healing every single day. Sit down with your kids and talk through how all of you feel. Mr. Rogers said it best, "Feelings are mentionable and manageable." God gives you all the tools you need to manage your emotions. You control your thoughts, so take charge of your thought life. Be intentional. Consider the blessings in your life. Think hope-filled thoughts.

From this day forward, frame every story to work for you, to strengthen you, to take you closer to who you want to be. You are choosing to grow and flourish from the inside out. Are you letting people off the hook who may have hurt you? No. You're obeying God's Word. "Beloved, never avenge yourselves, but leave it to the wrath of God, for it is written, 'Vengeance is mine, I will repay, says the Lord'" (Rom 12:19, ESV). Let God take care of them. He will. We have too many wonderful things ahead to spend one more minute mulling over the hurtful part of the past.

ACTION STEP:

Prepare to share your new story with friends. As you share, you will get stronger. Make sure you smile. Your life is a work in progress, just like everyone else's (even the Facebook/Instagram picture-perfect family). You must leave your old story behind. That's not you anymore. You are moving forward. Good things are coming your way, and you don't have time for pity parties or anger. You have an adventurous life to live and amazing family and friends to pour into. Your pain can translate into your purpose and calling. Make your disappointments and tragedies the springboard for your success. Think about every good thing that has happened since you made the decision to grow.

Write your story, your beautiful story. Tell it in a way that strengthens you. Say it out loud. Share it. You will get stronger by the day. This is your path. Choose life. Choose joy. Choose healing.

$\mathcal{D}$ay 5

FORGIVE

To be a Christian means to forgive the inexcusable because God has forgiven the inexcusable in you. — *C.S. Lewis*

God sent His only son to die for our sins. "For God so loved the world that He gave His only begotten son that whoever believes in Him should not perish but have everlasting life" (John 3:16). The most incredible act of love was forgiveness of our sins through Jesus' death on the cross. A constant awareness of this sacrificial act of love on our behalf keeps a heart humble and thankful. We are then able to extend forgiveness and love without judgement to others.

There is healing in forgiveness, and a healed heart is a hope-filled heart. Keep your heart soft and allow God to replace bitterness and unforgiveness with His beautiful, strengthening, steadfast love. Unforgiveness is the second unpardonable sin that isn't talked about often. God says He cannot forgive us if we don't forgive our brother. "For if you forgive other people when they sin against you, your heavenly Father will also forgive you. But if you do not forgive others, your Father will not forgive you your sins" (Matthew 6:14-15). Forgive those who have hurt you. Your own relationship with God depends on it. God has commanded that we forgive, and therefore forgiveness is an act of love – and obedience.

Forgiveness will keep a heart free from anger and make room for love. Make peace with your past so that you can own your future. Re-writing hurtful situations is one of the greatest gifts you can give yourself. Forgiveness will open your heart to a big, beautiful future filled with opportunities for a wonderful life. There is a deep connection between forgiveness and hope. I once heard someone say, "I really have a hard time forgiving someone who does me wrong." This mindset stems from pride and an underestimation of how many times people have had to forgive you when you have been the offender. Forgiveness is an act of love and humility. We humbly forgive knowing that we ourselves need God's forgiveness. Get rid of any feeling that pulls you backwards. Forgiveness is forward thinking. Only you can do this work. Make the decision today, and start building the muscle of forgiveness in your life. You will be a markedly happier person.

SISTERS

My sister and I shared a room our entire childhood. Mom would announce it was time for bed and Carrie and I would race to our beds. I think it became our last giggling moment of the day. We had this rule that the last one in bed had to go back and turn off the light. You know this was serious business, possibly life or death, depending on the size of the monsters under our beds. Clearly, the last one to bed, now that the light was out, would be the most likely to be eaten by those monsters. You know what I'm saying. Don't act like you didn't leap from a little distance when you got close to your bed, just in case.

Every night before we fell asleep, we had another rule. We had to ask one another for forgiveness for any anger or ugliness. Being 12 months and 3 weeks apart, we had our little disagreements. Sometimes I acted like the oldest and sometimes she did. Most nights, we would take turns being the one to lead in forgiveness. We would say, "Hey, I'm sorry we had a fight today," or "I'm sorry if I hurt your feelings today." And the other would always reply, "Me too. I'm sorry too." We'd exchange I love you's and our goodnights, and we'd go to sleep.

That was one of the most powerful habits of my childhood — forgiveness before bed.

"In your anger do not sin; do not let the sun go down while you are still angry, and do not give the devil a foothold" (Ephesians 4:26-27). This Scripture could not be any clearer. Never go to bed angry. You will allow Satan a foothold in your life. I've seen this play out so many times. I saw an interview with an older couple who had been married 75 years. When asked how they stayed married for so long, they responded, "We don't always agree, but we do agree that we work it out before we go to sleep. Some nights are very long, but we refuse to go to bed angry."

FORGIVENESS IN DIVORCE

One of the most difficult challenges in my life was suddenly becoming a single mom. As of 2019, out of 130 countries, the United States had the world's highest rate of children living in single-parent homes. Twenty-three percent of children under the age of 18 live with one parent in the U.S., as opposed to 7 percent around the rest of the world. If you're a single parent, I don't have to tell you how challenging this role is. *How do I work full time and make sure I'm home for the kids? How do I divide my time with the kids and the other parent in a way that they grow up emotionally healthy? How do I fill the role of mom and dad? Am I enough?* Of all the challenges of a single parent, one of the most important and impactful acts of love for your children is to forgive the other parent.

I have two sons. Their father and I divorced when the boys were 12 and 14 years old. I'm thankful that today, the boys' father and I have a good relationship. And by good, I mean we can still make one another laugh. For instance, the other day I texted him about ideas for a new domain name. I said, "Hey, you're the computer guru, what domain name do you think I should look for?" His lovely response, "Well, how about MarlaTalks.com or MarlaWon'tShutUp.com?" followed by three little laughy faces. I sent back a couple of eye-rolling GIFs, and then he was kind to help me. Learning to laugh again didn't happen overnight, but I'm so thankful it happened. Peace and forgiveness after a divorce is a beautiful thing for everyone.

"Therefore, if you are offering your gift at the altar and there remember that your brother or sister has something against you, leave your gift there in front of the altar. First go and be reconciled to them; then come and offer your gift" (Matthew 5:23-24). Unforgiveness will put distance between you and God and your ability to hear clearly from Him. Forgiveness is incredibly freeing and humbling. Walking in forgiveness, you lay a strong foundation for God to do amazing things in your life. You will hear from God and be forgiven of your own sin. To walk in forgiveness after a divorce will bring healing to your heart and to the hearts of your children.

Never forget who the real enemy is. If your heart is broken because you just experienced a curve ball in life, don't forget who the pitcher is. The pitcher is not your ex, your boss, or your co-worker. The real enemy is the one who wants to steal your life. "For our struggle is not against flesh and blood but against the rulers, against the authorities, against the powers of this dark world and against the spiritual forces of evil in the heavenly realms" (Ephesians 6:12). Don't forget who is really against you. The enemy wants you angry and bitter. He wants you to hold on to resentment and hatred. Whatever you do, don't let him win. "I tell you, love your enemies and pray for those who persecute you" (Matthew 5:44). The harder Satan pushes, the harder we should love. Forgiveness is not forgetting; it's remembering without anger. The healthier your view of your past, the better your future will be. God can help you forgive, but the decision is yours to make. Martin Luther King, Jr. said, "Forgiveness is not an occasional act, it is a constant attitude."[10]

MOM FORGAVE HER DAD

One of the most beautiful acts of forgiveness I've ever witnessed was between my mom and her father. You see, my grandpa was a mean man when he drank (and that was often). He was an alcoholic. My grandma loved him very much and had three children with him. He didn't come home very often and when he did, he was usually intoxicated and it was scary for the family. Recently I heard a few more stories from my mom's childhood, and it was all I could do not to cry. It is difficult for me to comprehend a family life like that, as my father was nothing but loving and kind.

Grandpa and Grandma eventually divorced when their children were all teenagers. He moved in with another lady, and my mom and her siblings did not see him much after that. All three children grew up, married, and had children of their own. I'm still amazed at how loving and close all of our family is to this day. Grandma will tell you it was all Jesus. Grandma loved and prayed for each one of us. She was the anchor. She always kept unity and love the priority. I spent many weekends with Grandma, and I always loved to hear her call out every family member's name in prayer before bed. Her prayers saved our family.

I remember my mom and dad trying to find Grandpa at Christmastime because mom always wanted to share Jesus with him. Sometimes we would find him and have dinner with him, and then he'd be gone again. I only remember seeing him maybe two or three times as a young girl.

I moved to Missouri to go to college and would go back home to Oklahoma to see my family. One summer, Mom told me that she needed to go find Grandpa because she heard he was in financial trouble. He had given his landlord my mom's contact information, and the landlord called to let her know he was being evicted. My mom and I found him. It was then, that he came home to live with Mom and Dad. He spent his final years on this earth being loved deeply by my parents. He lived with them four years until he was diagnosed with cancer. They loved and cared for him until his dying day.

My mom walked in forgiveness. Mom did everything she could do for her dad. She forgave her father, though he never asked. She forgave him because that's what God asked her to do. She forgave him and I saw the love of Jesus as I watched my mom love a dad who had been anything but loving to her. I saw God's love through my mom's heart toward her father.

Maybe there is someone you need to forgive. We have all been there. Pray until your heart is soft again. Pray until you feel God replace every bit of anger with love. He will do that. If someone hurt you and they aren't a part of your life any-more, you can still ask God to heal your heart, and He will. Not looking back with regret, we are choosing love. God can give you a soft heart to build a beautiful future. His loving kindness will give you peace and joy and heal your hurts. All we have to do is accept His love. Never fight to hang on to feelings that hurt you. You have a choice, and you can choose healing and God's sweet peace.

GRACE TO FORGIVE A RAPIST

The story of Helen Roseveare, missionary to the Congo, is another example of what true forgiveness looks like. Helen grew up in England, graduated from Cambridge with her degree in medicine, and felt called to the Congo to help establish medical facilities. In March of 1953, at the age of 28, she arrived in the northeastern region of the Congo (Zaire).[11]

In 1964, Civil War broke out. All of the medical facilities that Helen had spent years building were destroyed. Ten protestant missionaries were imprisoned, including Helen. It was then that Helen was brutally raped. On October 29, 1964, she wrote, "On that dreadful night, beaten and bruised, terrified and tormented, unutterably alone, I had felt at last God had failed me. Surely, He could have stepped in earlier, surely things need not have gone that far. I had reached what seemed to be the ultimate depth of despairing nothingness." In the middle of her darkness, Helen sensed the Lord speaking to her, "You asked Me, when you were first converted, for the privilege of being a missionary. This is it. Don't you want it? These are not your sufferings, they're Mine. All I ask of you is the loan of your body."

Helen recounts that she sensed an "overwhelming sense of privilege, that Almighty God would stoop to ask of me, a mere nobody in a forest clearing in the jungles of Africa, something He needed." She later journaled:

> Through the brutal heartbreaking experience of rape, God met with me – with outstretched arms of love. It was an unbelievable experience: He was so utterly there, so totally understanding, his comfort was so complete – and suddenly I knew – I really knew that his love was unutterably sufficient. He did love me! He did understand! I knew that "My God will supply every need of yours according to his riches in glory in Christ Jesus" (Philippians 4:19) was true on all levels, not just on a hyper-spiritual shelf where I had tried to relegate it...He was actually offering me the inestimable privilege of sharing in some little way in the fellowship of His sufferings.

Helen gave a beautiful challenge to choose healing when she shared her Urbana '76 Address:

One word became unbelievably clear, and that word was privilege. He didn't take away pain or cruelty or humiliation. No! It was all there, but now it was altogether different. It was with him, for him, in him. In the weeks of imprisonment that followed and in the subsequent years of continued service, looking back, one has tried to "count the cost," but I find it all swallowed up in privilege. The cost suddenly seems very small and transient in the greatness and permanence of the privilege.

Helen went on to establish a new 250-bed medical center in Zaire. She wrote several books and served as a missionary advocate until she went to be with the Lord, for whom she counted it a privilege to suffer, on December 7, 2016, at the age of 91.

God help us to leave legacies of forgiveness like Helen. The moment she decided to walk in forgiveness she opened the door for God to use her story for decades, sharing hope with thousands upon thousands of people.

ACTION STEP:

Today is the day to forgive. Forgiveness opens the door for hope. It's your turn. Whom do you need to forgive today? Someone in your past, someone you live with, a friend, a relative, yourself? Please don't move on to Chapter 6 until you say a prayer and ask God to help you forgive. Make a decision right now, in this very moment, to choose forgiveness. I'm so excited for the beautiful life that you will live on the other side of forgiveness. Be brave.

Day 6

POWERFUL PROGRESS

Failure is success in progress.
— Albert Einstein

B ack home in Oklahoma we had a special phrase to describe disappointment or a feeling we just couldn't put into words. I'm pretty sure you won't hear it at the Royal Palace, but this phrase says it all, "Well I'll be daaaaaaaagum." Do you ever look back over your life and think, Hmmm? I just say, "Well I'll be daaaaaaaagum." I think that phrase is a great summation of all of the ups and downs of life. We all know we're not perfect. We will make mistakes. We won't hit the mark every time. You know the drill: it's not how many times you fall, it's how many times you get back up. Fall down seven times, get up eight. I have a theory. Every time you fall, make sure you fall forward, so when you get up, you're still closer to your goal.

When something doesn't go as planned, slow down, and assess what went down and why. Ask God for wisdom to learn the lesson. Lessons in life will be repeated until they are learned. Keep in mind there is a bigger picture. The enemy will use absolutely anything to take you down mentally and make you feel like you just can't make the cut, or you never get it right and you never will. Such a lie is straight from "h-e-double hockey sticks." The enemy will use any situation to keep you from running toward your goals and accomplishing all of the amazing things that only you can do. Don't you dare let him win. When the enemy pushes you, push back harder. When the enemy tries to discourage me, I find something I can do for God and take it up a notch. I say out loud, "Oh, you messed with the wrong girl this time."

Saying YES to Progress

Remember youth camp and the awesome speakers who told stories you'll remember until Jesus returns? One summer, a special speaker asked everyone to take out a piece of paper. At the top of the paper, we had to write, "Dear God." Then, she asked if we would be willing to say yes to anything God asked of us. Whatever it looked like, would we say yes? If so, we had to write a big, fat YES right in the middle of the page and then sign it. I remember thinking that day, God, whatever you call me to, please help me to always answer YES!

Right now, you are holding in your hands one of those yesses. I'm bringing you along with me. We're on a mission to keep showing up, flaws and all, and say YES to the Lord. We are committed to obedience and walking with God through every high and every low. When you're attacked and things don't go like you thought they would, stay the course. Every day, say YES to God, and you will make progress. This reminds me of a Holly Hobbie notebook I had in third grade. The bright red cover read, "Please be patient with me, God isn't finished with me yet." We are all a work in progress. God will use the heart that says, "Yes! Count me in!"

A Special Song

Over the course of my life, I have found that if I made myself available, God always opened a door for me. Sometimes, I would think to myself, *Why are you saying yes to this? Have you lost your ever-lovin' mind, Marla?* (Did I mention I'm an Okie?) And then the Lord would remind me of a prayer I prayed often as a teenager, "Here am I, Lord. Send me!"

I always loved to sing. I sang in the church choir. I sang in the school choir. Somehow, I always had solos — and, something would always happen to keep me humble. Let's see, there was the time I stood before a congregation of 3,000 church family members as a teen. I was supposed to sing a solo part, and the 300-member choir would repeat the last line of each of the verses I sang. I opened my mouth to sing my solo part and my mind went completely blank. I could not remember one word. Not one. I panicked. I did not know what to do, so I did what came to my mind first. I made up every single word to a nice little ditty about how good God was. I think I might have even sung, "God is great, God is good, and we thank Him for this food." I was trying to think of every spiritual word I'd ever heard in my whole life. I tried to sing Bible verses. Anything that sounded remotely Christian-ese, I sang it. Mama-mia, it was rough! Absolutely none of the choir's memorized lines made sense anymore. There was a little part of me that wanted to pretend like my song was the real song and the whole choir forgot their part. Nope. It was me — aaaaall me. I. Messed. Up. Again. Now what? Would I put myself in this position again? Here's my answer: "Then Jesus told his disciples a parable to show them that they should always pray and not give up" (Luke 18:1). I wasn't giving up.

I was completely shocked every single time another opportunity came my way. I would be asked to do something important or really big (in my mind), and I would think, *Do*

*they not know? How is this opportunity even coming my way?
What if I screw up again?* I kept the little rule I had made
for myself: if it was in my ability to ever do something for
Jesus, something that could impact others and bring glory to
God, my answer would be YES hands-down, every time. I
decided a long time ago, I would never say no just because I
was afraid. I decided as a young girl that if God entrusted me
with an assignment, fear was not an option, no way, no how,
not now, not ever.

High School Musical

I was so excited to be part of the high school musical. I even
had a solo. I was ready to go. I had my black leggings, a big
overshirt, a five-inch wide belt, and, of course, my 5-inch heels.
It was the cutest little '80s outfit you ever did see. Oh, and let's
not forget, I had used almost a whole can of the finest Aqua
Net hairspray ever made (and that was just for my bangs).

It was time — the moment I had prepared for all year. The
curtain came up. There I was on the six-foot-elevated plat-
form. It was my moment to shine in front of all of my peers.
My singing debut! The spotlight came on, and I sang my heart
out. The crowd cheered. The spotlight went off, and I was to
exit stage right. I had to hurry before the next act would be in
place and the lights would come back on. Did I mention how

bright the spotlight was? Have you ever had someone shine a flashlight in your eyes and all you could see was white spots for the next 500 hours? That's what it was like. You guessed it. I COULDN'T SEE ONE THING. I knew when the light came back on, the next act would be on stage, and I would be standing there with my arms stretched out, fumbling in the air like a baby learning to walk. I had to get off the stage. I had seconds to figure this out, so I did the only logical thing I could think to do. I just walked. Oh sure, that sounds easy enough if you're heading in the right direction. But what if, in the dark, you get turned around and, oh, let's say you're facing the back of the stage — you know where it drops six feet to the ground? And — you just walk. I can tell you what happens next. You walk right off the six-foot drop. The best part? My mic was still on when I hit the ground. Yep, the audience may not have seen it, but they sure heard it. Every time I replay that whole thing in my head, I just wish I hadn't grunted when I hit the ground, or at least didn't have the mic next to my mouth when I landed.

The show ended, and I was hoping that no one heard. Yeah, right! Everyone ran up to hug the performers afterward. I wasn't sure if I should mention it. I mean, maybe no one heard. Then came that wonderful moment mom walked up to hug me and said, "Honey you did so good — but what was that loud noise when you left the stage?" Yeah, so, there's that.

Maybe you "went for it" and did a thing, and you didn't exactly rock at it. Welcome to the club, my friend. I love how Michael Jordan put it, "I've missed more than 900 shots in my career. I've lost almost 300 games. Twenty-six times, I've been trusted to take the game-winning shot and missed. I've failed over and over again in my life. And that is why I succeed." It's all about showing up anyway. For the most part, I can tell you something that didn't go right just about every time I have been on a stage or behind a mic. I had to learn to laugh at myself, get better, and grab the mic afraid. Sometimes I have to remind myself, *Obey God, Marla. He said, "Do not be afraid; do not be discouraged" (Deut. 31:8). It's not about you.*

ONE AMAZING AUCTION

I hadn't spoken at very many events, but when I was asked, you know what my answer was. My answer was, "YES! Of course, I'll speak at the ladies' luncheon at the church! I'll share my heart and change lives for Jesus! Yes! Yes! Yes!" The day came, and the lovely luncheon was happening. I was introduced. I held the microphone and passionately shared my heart. I told all of the ladies about an upcoming opportunity to help children in our community. I held back tears as I shared the heart of the local baseball team that was joining our efforts. "Ladies, these men are so committed to helping our kids. They believe so much in these kids, they're actually going all out this year and auctioning their balls at our next event!" All of a sudden, I hear a chuckle from one of the tables. I thought, *What in the world? There is nothing funny about that?* And I'm actually teary-eyed as I'm sharing the hearts of these players. I thought perhaps they misunderstood me. So, guess what? I REPEATED IT. "I just can't believe these guys are such givers. I can't believe the team is joining our mission and auctioning their balls!" They were laughing harder now and I just thought maybe something else funny happened in the room so YOU GUESSED IT...I REPEATED IT AGAIN. By now, several tables were laughing and I could see the laughter was spreading across the room. In my head I was going over and over what I had just said while trying to keep talking to the audience, when — it hit me. I needed to add one little word "BASE" to the word "BALL." Too late. I lost the crowd. Let's just say, I was never asked to speak at the Annual Ladies Luncheon at the church ever again.

RADIO

I could go on and on about the mistakes I've made behind a mic. The fact that I host a radio show just adds to the beauty of knowing God can use anyone and will bless your commitment to serve Him. Just keep showing up. God will keep opening doors. He didn't keep track of all the times I failed. He never once said to me, "Oh Marla, too many blunders, go home!" I kept watching Him open doors for me, and I kept saying YES, even when I was afraid of another fail. Keep saying yes to God. Let Him do the refining. Allow God to take you where He wants you. He always has the best plan. Keep showing up. Keep working hard. He will put you right where you need to be. He will bless your obedience.

LAUGHTER IS PROGRESS

"A cheerful heart is good medicine, but a crushed spirit dries up the bones" (Proverbs 17:22). When you miss the mark, choose to laugh. The goal is to learn from our mistakes. Learning to laugh saves you from a crushed spirit. Making people laugh is a ministry of healing. It's up to us to use every opportunity to grow, to bring glory to God, and keep going. Don't shrink back because you didn't give the perfect delivery. Get stronger, and prepare to kill it on your next go-around.

Learning to laugh at yourself is a sign that you forgive yourself. Forgiveness is a kindness you show yourself. You have a choice. Either laugh and heal, or choose discouragement and waste away. Choose laughter; choose healing.

Keep reminding yourself that you are making progress even when you don't hit the mark. You will get better every time you show up. Be passionate about every opportunity. Not one of us has ever gotten it right every time. Settle in your heart that you are a work in progress, a masterpiece in the making.

Obedience

When God is doing something new in your life, never look back. You don't have to remind Him that last time really didn't work out so well, or of how incompetent you are, or how you messed up royally before. Remember what happened to Lot's wife? "Flee for your lives. Don't look back" (Gen. 19:17). "But Lot's wife looked back, and she became a pillar of salt" (Gen. 19:26). For Lot's wife, it was a matter of life and death. It is for us, too. God knows exactly what He's doing. Be courageous, don't look back, trust Him with your "yes," and prepare for the next beautiful thing in your life. It will come.

Lot's wife was disobedient and the cost was her life. God told her not to look back. He warned, and she had a choice. "Remember Lot's wife" (Luke 17:32)! There are consequences for disobedience. Like a friend of mine once said, "You can choose your sin, but you can't choose your consequence." Disobedience will affect more than just you. We will never know what blessings would have been a part of Lot's wife's life, had she obeyed. Her decision left her children to grow up without their mom.

There is blessing on the other side of your YES. Remember, Joseph said YES to God and went from being a slave to second in command of all of Egypt. Moses said YES to following the cloud by day and the pillar of fire by night. Mary said YES to giving birth to Jesus Christ. God loves to bless obedience. Imagine what's on the other side of your YES!

IN THE WAIT

Abraham Lincoln once said, "The best way to predict your future is to create it." Do every single thing in your power to do, and watch God multiply your efforts and do what only He can do. Some things you can't make happen, but there are some things that only you can make happen. Every decision matters. It's about how you're spending your time, your precious moments of your day. Make the decisions that help you to be your best self, the hard decisions that will help you conquer your goals. Eat well. Make time for rest and exercise. Be kind to yourself and others.

As you seek God, you will get stronger and more attuned to His voice. He will give you shortcuts. He will bring blessing your way. God's blessing is worth the wait, every time. Look for ways to walk in obedience. While writing this book, I would spend my evenings in prayer, and during those times, God would give me a vision for what I was to share in this book. He would give me stories and speak to my heart. He will do that for you. As you get closer to Him, He will speak to you and give you supernatural insight. You may accomplish goals in half the time. You may see double blessings in your finances or your relationships. God even did amazing things in my personal relationships during the time I was writing this book about hope. Trust His timing. "He has made everything beautiful in its time." (Ecclesiastes 3:11) Every single time God mentions "waiting" on Him, the result is always good. Don't rush and settle. Wait for God's best.

PROGRESS IN THE FAIL

Divorce? Not even on my radar. I grew up planning my whole life out; not kidding. I took that whole "failing to plan is a plan to fail" thing seriously — for real. I knew the year I was going to marry. I knew how many children I would probably have. I was pretty sure I knew what gender they would be and how splendid our home life would be. I knew what my husband's work hours would be and had a pretty good idea of the meals I would cook every night when he got home at 5:45 p.m. And then there would be the moment we would all sit down to hold hands and pray before we partook of the evening meal at 6:30 p.m. Yeah, right! I guess you see where I'm going with that. My life did not look anything like I thought it would. Some parts of my life were better than I had imagined, and other parts were more challenging than I would have ever thought. Let God lead, and trust Him as you walk in obedience, following everything written in His Word.

Remember that illustration of that plane ride to a great destination in the Introduction of this book? At some point on a plane ride that I get so excited about, I begin to check my watch. My legs begin to stiffen up and I feel like I need fresh air. I want to go for a walk but can't. I'm uncomfortable and the minutes are passing so slowly I feel like I'm in a time warp. I'm still heading toward an amazing destination, but at some point, I have to stay in my seat and stop thinking of all the things I don't like on this plane. It's my responsibility to control my thoughts. I have to make the decision to think about the good things that are on the other side of this temporary, uncomfortable season I'm in. At this moment, I can encourage the person next to me. I can speak life on this long plane ride and be a light. I can be productive on this flight. This is no time to bail and, besides, that isn't an option. Don't give up when you cannot see your destination out your plane window. You're still heading in the right direction. Trust God while you're in the air and the view looks pretty much the same in every direction with no sign of a sandy beach in sight.

You may be on the longest plane ride of your life, but keep your head. Look for the beauty that is all around you. Who are you traveling with? Enjoy those people, appreciate them, and thank God for them. Your thoughts are your choice. When you can't see a beautiful landing in sight, trust God, your pilot. He will get you there. Put your hope in God!

WHEN IT'S OUT OF YOUR CONTROL

Wait! Hold everything. This was not my plan. Can't somebody make this stop? It felt like a bad dream, and I couldn't wait to wake up. But no. I had two options. Keep moving or die. There were days I didn't think I had a choice. I was pretty sure I was going to die from a broken heart. I fasted and prayed and fasted and prayed, and he got married again, but not to me. The miracle wasn't going to be the one I was praying for. It was all about trusting God.

What did I do with my broken heart? I ran to the church. I didn't miss one service. I watched God give me peace in the storm. He was so faithful to provide all that I needed, a great job, food on the table, and more. Then one night, as I was reading, I found the verse I would stand on until He healed my heart. "The Lord is good to those whose hope is in Him, to the one who seeks Him, it is good to wait quietly for the salvation of the LORD" (Lamentations 3:25-26). God healed my heart. I could love my children's new stepmom. I knew God would take care of me if I kept my heart soft and trusted Him with my future — and He has. God has been so good to me. Winston Churchill said it best, "The ability to move from failure to failure with no loss of enthusiasm makes you a champion."

God promised to be good to those whose hope is in Him. There is a battle for your hopes. Satan wants you to hope in everything but God (money, children, spouse, relationships, friends). Ask yourself if there is something you may be putting your hope into more than God. The enemy loves to distract and put counterfeits on our path. As we focus on God, He will focus on our miracles.

We have a job to do while we are hoping and waiting. God asked us to seek Him and wait quietly for His salvation. He promises to rescue us, and He cannot lie. He promises that when we run after Him, He will always take care of us. He will be good to us if we wait quietly. A good prayer is, *God help me to be wise and patient, trusting you with every season of my life.*

It doesn't matter how far away you are from your original plan. God's plan today is far better than any of your plans yesterday. Start right where you are, ask God for help, and watch Him intervene. God doesn't run out of plans. And the best news of all: His plans will succeed. Starting today, get ready for His new plan for your life and don't fight it. Resistance to a different plan will wear you down. Open your heart to enjoy a future that will be better than you can imagine. Let go of the past, take a deep breath, and be all-in, ready to say yes to your new journey filled with hope. Lift your head. Put those shoulders back. Follow God's orders, and prepare for success.

COMEBACKS

It was 1938, and the world renowned pistol shooter, Karoly Takacs, had won many championships.[12] During a training session in the army, a grenade exploded in his right hand, completely destroying it. Takacs believed that since he still had his left hand, he would learn to shoot with it. After one year of training with his left hand, he competed in the Hungarian national shooting championship and won. He went on to compete in the 1948 Olympics and won the gold medal.

Imagine yourself as a Karoly. Your right hand represents the original plan of your life — the most amazing plan in the history of all plans. The plan was as perfect as Karoly's right-handed shooting, and you would have won championships with that plan. Then, life happens, and your right hand (perfect plan) is completely destroyed. At this very moment, you are Karoly. Are you going to start practicing to shoot with your left hand and win championships, or not? Better yet, I love that he perfected his new way of shooting in less than a year. We can't become a good left-handed shooter if we're too busy crying over losing the original, right-handed plan. You have championships to win with your left hand. What are you waiting for?

Consistent Progress

James Clear said, "Ultimately, it is your commitment to the process that will determine your progress."[13] Be committed. Be consistent. Consistent progress stirs hope. Making progress every day, no matter how small, will get you to the goal. You decide how quickly, but don't let a day go by without making a move in the right direction. I have relationships that I want to be strong. Every day I look for ways to build and strengthen them. That goes for my family and God. Good relationships are a top priority, and consistent, loving habits will strengthen any relationship.

Whatever your goal may be, start today and make one tiny step in that direction. Your step may be as small as writing down your goal or maybe sharing your goal with someone close to you. Start today, and consistently move in the direction of your dreams.

Research shows that having a friend as an accountability partner will increase your rate of success when implementing new habits. I have a friend that I've been doing life with for over 20 years. We inspire, encourage, and challenge one another to be better than we were yesterday. Pray for a friend like that. God will answer.

GRATITUDE

A thankful heart is a hope-filled heart. A recent study showed that grateful individuals experience more positive emotions, are more satisfied with life, and experience fewer negative emotions including depression, anxiety and envy.[14] They are also more likely to be empathetic, forgiving, helpful, and supportive than those who are less grateful. The study also found that grateful people tend to be more spiritually and religiously minded.

Make a list of the good things that have happened since a major painful event in your life, and you will see how God has provided. Your list might include things like a new job, a new place to live, more time with your children, more time with God, new friends (like your new BFF, Marla), better eating habits, a new fitness regimen. Look at all of those miracles! Don't forget to celebrate the miracles!

ACTION STEP:

It's time for your comeback! Spend a few moments today taking an honest look at your life. Maybe you've been on auto-pilot and you realize you can actually take hold of the steering wheel and head exactly where you want to go. As you seek God and trust the doors He is opening and closing, prepare for an incredible life. He loves to give us gifts. He wants to bless you. Miracles will come your way when you choose to follow Him and trust the process. Start today by praising God for the miracles you haven't even seen yet. Just think, this is only day six, and hope is already at work in your life.

Day 7

ELIMINATION

Clutter is not just an accumulation of stuff –
it's anything that stands between you and a bigger life.

Clutter can accumulate in many places. Eliminate clutter and you will eliminate a major source of anxiety. Tackle it. Control it, and you will immediately give yourself room for a bigger life filled with hope. Living clutter-free is a lifestyle. Every day there will be opportunity to let it creep in or keep it in its place (no pun intended). I cannot put enough emphasis on the value of clutter-control. A few places to watch for this sneaky little tormentor are your home, your office, your car, your calendar, and your mind.

Clutter will lead to a loss of time, your most valuable commodity — the one commodity that once lost you can never get back. The less you deal with clutter, the more time you will have to build your life. You will actually add space to your day by keeping clutter at bay. It's time to let go of distractions and go after your spiritual, relational, physical, and financial goals.

IT STARTS AT HOME

This isn't a chapter on housekeeping. It goes much deeper than that. There's a reason our highly trained military start their day by making their bed and insist on impeccably clean barracks. Admiral William McRaven said it best, "If you make your bed every morning you will have accomplished the first task of the day. It will give you a small sense of pride and it will encourage you to do another task and another and another. By the end of the day, that one task completed will have turned into many tasks completed. Making your bed will also reinforce the fact that little things in life matter. And if by chance, you have a miserable day, you will come home to a bed that is made, that you made. And a made bed gives you encouragement that tomorrow will be better."[15] As you create order and accept full responsibility for your environment, you open the door to accomplish bigger goals. Orderly barracks and homes keep your mind free of excess weight, the weight of clutter. When you choose hope-filled action steps, you are choosing life.

Removing clutter and keeping order in your home is essential for building your future. The ripple effect will change the lives of those around you. Your home should be a place of order, peace, and flow.

When the boys were little, I loved spontaneous trips with them. The more orderly our house was, the more easily we could pack up and head out for a good time with friends, go for a swim, or enjoy a day at the local theme park. Clothes were clean and put away, and we could readily find anything we needed. Everyone thrives when there is order, but the lack thereof is frustrating for everyone. Clutter and disorder will disrupt the flow and peace in your home.

Training your children to keep their rooms orderly will help train them to keep their lives orderly. Both of my boys are grown now and they both love a clean home. There is a wonderful sense of accomplishment when there is order in a home. Make it a family affair to keep order. Work together, and make it enjoyable for everyone. Play music, and set a timer for each area that needs cleaning. Commit to one or two rooms, have a snack break, and repeat with the next room. Make it fun.

Take a look around you. What areas seem to pile up in your home? Stop and fix it. Call a friend and ask for suggestions, or search the web for organization possibilities. Don't ignore the issue; resolve it. Don't let another day go by without addressing the parts of your home that create anxiety.

With a little attention, most of these issues can be addressed and fixed. Do you remember the verse, "Cleanliness is next to godliness?" Me neither. That's because it's not a Bible verse, but you couldn't convince my grannie of that.

I remember a good friend and her family stopping by one evening. I had no idea they were coming over. We enjoyed a wonderful visit. Out of nowhere, she asked, "Were you expecting company tonight?"

I said, "No. Why do you ask?"

She smiled, "Well, your house is so clean, candles lit and lamps on everywhere."

I said, "Oh, this is just how I like to spend the evenings." For me, it was all about the peace and quiet in my home that led to peace and quiet in my soul. I loved to sit on the couch with the boys on either side of me, and we would look at the latest edition of "Guinness Book of World Records," or we'd try to find all of the items in our latest "I Spy" book. Those are precious moments I will always cherish. Quiet, peaceful evenings with my two favorite gifts on the planet. I wouldn't trade the crazy times either, like the times they surprised me with snakes they had caught and couldn't wait to run in and show me the lizards dangling from their earlobes.

We didn't usually have a TV on at our house. I loved that the boys led their own adventures outside. Exploring the great outdoors encouraged creativity. They built their own zoo in the garage, complete with several aquariums filled with lizards, snakes, crawfish, turtles, and much more. A clutter-free environment will encourage imagination and creativity.

LAUNDRY

Another rule in life that is guaranteed to bring hope your way is *manage your laundry*. There are several rules you can establish right away. I have seen laundry overwhelm the best of the best.

1. Never let dirty laundry pileup. Stay on top of it.
2. Never go to bed with laundry in the washer or dryer. Wash, dry, and put away on the same day.
3. Only commit to one or two loads per day, or as many as you are able to see through to completion. You may or may not have a set laundry day.
4. Never leave a clean load of clothes in a pile on a table or a couch. Always finish the laundry load before bed.

I'm a firm believer that mismanaged laundry is one of the main causes of family drama. I don't have all the data collected to prove that, but I have a few friends who would agree. Set a few house rules, and bring order to a chore that will always be a part of family life.

Office

The same rules apply to your office (home or away). After researching the data, both Princeton and Harvard Universities agree that the human brain craves order. According to "The Case for Finally Cleaning Your Desk"[16] by Libby Sander, it is estimated that the average worker loses two hours a week searching for files and documents. Billions of dollars every year are spent on workplace stress. A recent study found that when participants cleared clutter from their work environments, they were better able to focus and process information, and their productivity increased. The study also showed that if you eliminate clutter at work, you may even like your job more. If you need help organizing files, emails, and data, ask. Make time to bring order to your office this week. The peace is worth it. Create an appointment on your calendar to do regularly scheduled cleanup and stay on top of it. Then, enjoy your new peaceful office.

Car

Keeping your car clean (inside and out) is a healthy habit. Bacteria can actually accumulate in the car if not kept clean. If there are things that must stay in the car, invest in organizers and storage compartments. Loose items in the car can create a hazard for everyone in the case of a sudden stop. If you're like me, you spend a lot of time in the car, and keeping order in all of the places you spend time is a healthy habit.

You know those moments when everyone decides to go to lunch and they want to jump in your car? Here's to never spending 10 minutes apologizing over a messy car, ever again. Keep a clean car that you can be proud of. Establish car rules so that everyone can do their part to keep it clean. My father had a rule that everything must be taken out of the car before you leave the car. You will establish a great habit when you train your kids to do their part to keep the car clean, and everyone gets to enjoy the benefits.

Calendar

Make sure you only keep one calendar. Otherwise, you will spend valuable time syncing your calendars. While I love to hand write in a calendar, keeping my calendar on my phone is more efficient. I can easily switch appointment times or dates when necessary, and I love the alarm reminders. I always have my phone with me and can readily keep the calendar current. Family wall calendars are fun for kids to take part in keeping track of family activities. They can update the calendar with school functions, parties, etc. Parents, you can always take a photo of the family wall calendar and add new dates to your phone.

Eliminate clutter on your calendar. This move will cause you to make difficult choices. You will need to decide on your priorities and build a calendar that follows that. The more focused you are on your priorities, the more you will recognize everything else is a distraction. Before you add anything to your calendar, ask yourself, *Is this a priority in my life? Will this appointment keep me on track with my life goals and the people I want to impact, or will this be a distraction?* Make sure your calendar lines up with your life goals. Steer clear of an overcrowded calendar that leads to an overcrowded life.

I remember talking to my dad in my 20s and chatting about my busy schedule. His answer? "You know who makes that schedule, don't you?" Hmmm. "Well, Dad, good point." I haven't forgotten his pearls of wisdom. Breathing calmly in the day is important — and healthy. If your day is too full, it's time to eliminate. Remove the extras — and the supposedly urgent — to make room for the important.

Mind

Keep your mind free from the clutter of unnecessary distractions, and you will be free to dream and create. The elimination of mind-clutter is a powerful step. This step requires intentionality with your thought life. Five areas I want to commit to being all-in are:

- Prayer time and reading God's Word
- Family time
- Work hours
- 5-Hour Rule of learning
- Health and wellness

These are my five non-negotiables in my day. Learning to unplug after work is an art and a discipline. Learning to put your phone away during these times is critical. As those five non-negotiables happen in my life, I am more fulfilled because I'm doing what matters most to me.

There is a theory called the 80/20 Rule, which states that 80 percent of your success comes from 20 percent of what you do. The goal, then, would be to do more of what brings success and less of what keeps you distracted. Our goal during these 15 days is to get on track, make power moves, hope again, and succeed at the things that are important to us.

As you train yourself to be intentional with your thoughts, you will clear up clutter and be more focused on what's right in front of you. Be fully present with God, at home and in your work. You will experience peace when you bring order to your thought-life. Peace will lead to more meaningful days, and that, my friend, is a wonderful thing.

If something is causing tension in your life, address it. Craig Groeschel says, "Anxiety is a signal alerting you that it's time to pray!"[17] Spend time in prayer until you feel God's peace, and then proceed.

Mind-clutter can be managed. You may be able to write out your thoughts, or you may need to process with a friend. Perhaps you need to have a crucial conversation with someone to bring clarity. Do it. If something comes to your mind and you have the power to act immediately, do so. As you pray and ask God to help unclutter your mind, He will give you good ideas. Always follow peace. Watch for God to open doors and, perhaps, close a few. As you spend time with Him, He will order your steps. "The Lord makes firm the steps of the one who delights in him" (Psalm 37:23, ESV).

Enjoy the Pause

Look for opportunities in your day to enjoy silence. Those pauses give your brain an opportunity to hit reset and are necessary for a healthy mental state. I encourage you to involve nature in your day as often as possible. God specifically mentions the beauty of nature in His Word several times, nature is His gift to us. Stop and enjoy a flower or a tree. God created those for you! Taking a minute to pause and enjoy nature has a way of reminding you that He cares about the details and what's on your mind — all the things you care about. He wants you to cast your cares on Him and enjoy His blessings.

You may ask how mastering your day will bring hope. As you bring order to your day, you will discover hidden nuggets of time, untapped opportunities to enjoy meaningful moments. You will find space for gratitude, joy, and peace. "In his days may the righteous flourish, and peace abound, till the moon be no more" (Psalm 72:7, ESV). My prayer is that as you get closer to Jesus and discover deeper meaning in every day, your days will flourish. Merriam-Webster defines flourish as "to grow well, to be healthy, to be very successful, to do very well." It's time to flourish!

"Be careful, then, how you live – not as unwise but as wise, making the most out of every opportunity, because the days are evil. Therefore, do not be foolish, but understand what the Lord's will is" (Ephesians 5:15-17). Ask God to reveal any changes that you need to make. Ask Him to show you what is most important and how to balance work and family. God will give you wisdom and clarity to prioritize your time. Intentionality with your time will give you hope to accomplish goals and dreams.

ACTION STEP:

You may be keenly aware that more than one area of clutter needs to be tackled. Start with just one today. In the next 24 hours, organize one area of tangible clutter. Out of love, I would encourage you to take a look at your calendar. Find one thing that you could eliminate to make room for the important act of clearing clutter and making room for HOPE. You're going to love the big, deep breath that follows this action step.

Day 8

BUH-BYE STRESS

Sometimes the most productive thing you can do is relax.
— Mark Black

I t all started when I was chatting with a friend on speaker phone a few years ago. We got ready to hang up and, according to her, I said, "buuuuh-bye." Apparently, she and her husband were laughing so hard, she had to call me back to thank me. She has always laughed about how laid back I do life. I think that's all relative, but it's her perspective. Anyway, I think it's an appropriate name for this little chapter of chill.

That friend loves to make me laugh. She tells stories about my boys and me playing in the yard. Her version is that the boys would do something death-defying, and I would call out in a melodic Snow White voice, "Now boys, we mustn't do that." She does a whole skit of me disciplining my sons using a voice that's a cross between Carol Brady and Edith Bunker. As any mom knows, there's a time to breathe deeply and count backwards and a time to pray to God that there's chocolate somewhere in the house while you figure out parenting.

THE POWER OF ONE WORD

In 2017, Olivia Blair wrote an article titled, "Using the Word 'Stress' Less Could Actually Make You Less Stressed."[18] A few years ago, I noticed that the less I used the word stress, the more peace I felt in my life. That word did not fill my heart with hope, so I made a rule that I would not allow myself to use it.

This single word removes all feelings of joy and insinuates an out-of-control situation. Over-using the word stress can become a crutch. It can cause you to exaggerate circumstances and mismanage emotions that all could have been diffused if the stressor had been addressed quickly. The word stress gives more power to a negative feeling than the ability to course-correct. Instead of labeling your situation as stressful, stop and recognize your anxious feelings. When those feelings arise, stand on the Scripture, "Do not be anxious about anything, but in every situation, by prayer and petition, with thanksgiving, present your requests to God. And the peace of God, which transcends all understanding, will guard your hearts and your minds in Christ Jesus" (Phil. 4:6-7). Obedience is to put away anxious feelings, not to name them. Pray and ask God for help.

Remove the word stress from your conversations, and instead, recognize what you are truly feeling, perhaps, overwhelmed? Stop and bring order to your plan. Pray for self-control and navigate through your difficult situation quickly. Free your mind for more hope by removing this word from your life. I can attest to this.

PRIORITIZE

God is a God of order. "For God is not a God of disorder. He is a God of peace" (1 Cor. 14:33). We need to follow suit, preparing and prioritizing for success. In order to prepare for success, we have to know what it looks like. It doesn't mean you know the exact final outcome of everything in your life. It means there is an order to your focus. As you maximize your efforts in the order of your priorities, you will be focused on the things that are most important to you.

God will fly your plane to success if you allow Him to be the pilot. It is through Him we will experience the "peace that passes all understanding" (Phil. 4:6) and "joy unspeakable" (1 Pet. 1:8). Throughout Scripture, there is an emphasis on the following order: God, family, work/mission field, growth. Check your priorities. An honest look at the way you spend your day will reveal your true priorities.

There are several apps created to help you honestly assess your time management skills. You are required to log the activities of your entire day and then evaluate to see if you're spending your time on the things you value most. You will see exactly how much time and effort you put into your priorities and if they really are your priorities. Evaluating your day will help you make necessary changes to accomplish the goals and dreams you really want to come to fruition.

I enjoyed Gary Keller's (founder of Keller Williams) book, The One Thing.[19] One of his great quotes is, "Work is a rubber ball. If you drop it, it will bounce back. The other four balls, family, health, friends, integrity are made of glass. If you drop one of those, it will be irrevocably scuffed, nicked, perhaps even shattered." Gary states that multitasking is a lie. He encourages you not to be great at everything at the same time. He says that your life is always shifting. "Success is built sequentially. It's one thing at a time."

GOD

Our standard, the Word of God, gives us clarity for our number one mission. "Seek first the kingdom of God and his righteousness, and all these things will be given to you as well" (Matt. 6:33). When we put God above everything else, He takes care of everything else. "Delight yourself in the Lord, and he will give you the desires of your heart" (Ps. 37:4). Delight in Him and He will take care of you. That's a promise. He knows what you need. He wants you to have joy and peace. "Now to him who is able to do far more abundantly than all that we ask or think, according to the power at work within us" (Eph. 3:20). His plan is better than our best plan. It's a supernatural plan.

After an honest assessment of my day, I had to hit the reset button. I had always claimed I was like Paul. Praying without ceasing, all day long. Okay, great, but when did I make time to listen and get direction? When did all the noise stop so I could get clarity and hear His answer? When did I truly seek Him? This takes us back to our most important power move. We must set time aside for God. Since that decision to make an appointment in my day for God, I feel more hope and peace than I ever have. I've witnessed miracles and have direction in many areas of my life that I did not have before. If God is your first priority, make sure your daily schedule reflects intentional time to be with Him. Prayer is the path to victory.

Family

Noah heard from God. "But Noah found favor in the eyes of the Lord. Noah was a righteous man, blameless among the people of his time, and he walked faithfully with God" (Gen. 6:8-9). When you walk faithfully with God, He will give you supernatural answers to your prayers. He will honor your faithfulness to Him.

Noah's second priority was his family. Remember when God told him to build that ark and everyone thought he was crazy? They made fun of him. It had never even rained before, and God was telling him to build a boat to save him and his family. What a powerful message that God will give you direction and help you save your own family.

God will give you wisdom to know how to reach your family, what to say and what to do. Pray and wait. Never give up on God's ability and desire to answer your prayers for your family. Prayer moves the hand of God. Pray fervently and believe. "Confess to one another therefore your faults (your slips, your false steps, your offenses, your sins) and pray for one another, that you may be healed and restored. The earnest (heartfelt, continued) prayer of a righteous man makes tremendous power available (dynamic in its working)" (James 5:16, AMPC).

It's time to pray earnestly for our families. Pray for specific needs for each family member. Pray for unity. Go to battle on behalf of your children and watch God work. Quote Matthew 19:26 out loud, "With God all things are possible." Make your family a priority in prayer and in action. This looks different for everyone. Sometimes, it looks like dinner once a week with my adult sons. It may be a phone call or text with different family members during the week. A friend of mine once said, "The world would be a better place if everyone took care of their own family." Whether you are close to your family or there is disunity, start by making your family a priority in your prayer time. Maybe you have siblings that don't speak or a family member making poor choices with their life. Stop, drop, and pray. Use a prayer journal to list family members and your prayers for them. Give praise to God as He answers your requests. Pray for wisdom, and God will lead you. He will open doors of communication. It's time to do battle on our knees on behalf of our families. It's time to lead and stand in the gap for your family.

Work/Mission Field

Whether you are a stay-at-home mom or working at a job outside the home, commit your work to the Lord. Be the best at your job. Ask God for good ideas to do your job effectively and efficiently. Ask God to help you solve problems. Arrive early. Stay a little late. Pray for favor and the ability to accomplish the work at hand. Pray for your influence with fellow coworkers. Dedicate your work to the Lord and He will bless it. God can work through you and bless your leaders, your coworkers, your company, and your work.

Give God all of the glory. "Lord, you alone are my portion and my cup; you make my lot secure" (Psalm 16:5). Every good thing comes from God. Thank Him for every good idea He gives you. As you seek Him and His direction, He will work in you and through you. In sports, the guy who makes the basket always points to the guy who threw the ball to him, giving credit to him. When God allows a miracle to come through you, point to Him.

One of my first jobs did not exactly spark joy. I decided that I was creating my own joy or misery, so I decided to change my mindset. *This is where God has me. I will rejoice in this day and be glad in it.* I decided to be thankful and give God praise for my job, and work harder at it than I ever had. I remember doing a mundane task and smiling as I whispered, "as unto you Lord." All of a sudden, I had a spring in my step. It wasn't long until God moved me from that job to one that I loved. Then, there was the day I moved to one I loved even more than that one. It's a journey. Thank God every step of the way. Trust Him with your journey and the people you are influencing at your job or jobs along the way. "And so, from the day we heard, we have not ceased to pray for you, asking that you may be filled with the knowledge of His will in all spiritual wisdom and understanding, so as to walk in a manner worthy of the Lord, fully pleasing to Him: bearing fruit in every good work and increasing in the knowledge of God" (Col. 1:9-10, ESV).

Be the light. "Do all things without grumbling or questioning, that you may be blameless and innocent, children of God without blemish in the midst of a crooked and twisted generation, among whom you shine as lights in the world" (Phil. 2:14-15, ESV). Have a thankful heart in the mundane and you will spark joy everywhere you go. Speak kindly about those you work for and work with. Take joy with you, especially to your workplace. Pray for ways to enjoy your work and inspire those around you. Speak life into your coworkers. Encourage one another throughout your day. Arrive to work early and prepared. That alone will encourage your leaders. Punctuality shows a heart of respect for the company and will give you a peaceful start to your day. Don't miss a wonderful opportunity to be a blessing without saying a word.

Set goals at work. This will inspire you to grow and learn with a deadline. Work goals are important. Dedicate your work to the Lord, do everything as unto Him, and He will bless you. "Whatever you do, work at it with all your heart, as working for the Lord, not for human masters, since you know that you will receive an inheritance from the Lord as a reward. It is the Lord Christ you are serving" (Col. 3:23-24). Take your breaks, do something fun during your lunchtime, figure out how to enjoy your job. Be careful how you speak about your work. Be kind when speaking about your bosses and fellow employees. Lift your boss's arms. Help him carry his load. My daddy always said, "Never say an ugly word about a man who signs your paycheck." God sees and hears every conversation. Blessing will follow kind words and encouragement at your job. When you share joy at work, you're sharing hope. God will help you be a light in your mission field.

Never leave a job just because it's not fun. You be the one to spread joy at your job, and God will open doors and promote you. Make it a priority to study ways to be better at your job. Be the best in your field. Work excellently as unto the Lord in whatever you do. Put effort into it. Ask God to give you good ideas, and He will. Make your boss happy he hired you. Have an incredible work ethic. Use your time wisely at work. Be dependable, be responsible, and show up with a smile. Take hope to work.

Avoiding Decision Fatigue

Decision fatigue: A human's ability to make decisions can get worse after making so many decisions that the brain is fatigued. The goal should be to create systems and routines to eliminate as many decisions as possible in a day in order to avoid decision fatigue. Learning to streamline your workday, your morning routine, your bedtime routine — all of the non-negotiables in your day — will strengthen you. Routines actually create space in your day, which frees your mind to be more creative and problem solve.

Here are a few shortcuts you can implement right away. Some of these tips will relieve last-minute pressure from decision fatigue.

1. Schedule your bills to be automatically withdrawn from your bank account.
2. Fill your gas tank at the half-empty mark.
3. Always stop for gas on your way home from an event, never on your way to an event.
4. Keep your home in order, so you know where everything is and can get ready quickly.
5. Keep your closet in order. Rotate seasonal clothing (including shoes), ensuring you're only looking at current seasonal options.

6. Assess and find permanent places for items that may be piling up on a table or in any area of your home.

7. Purchase baskets or find a drawer, and create a system to avoid pileups. Go through mail the minute it comes in the house. Junk mail goes in the trash. Create a space for mail that needs to be addressed.

8. Create a space for things used daily, such as your keys, purse, and computer bag. They all should have designated places so they are easily grabbed on the go in the morning.

9. Make phone calls on speaker phone while cleaning or walking (great times for getting some cardio in).

10. Be very intentional with appointments, making sure to set start and stop times, including friend time.

11. Arrive 15 minutes prior to any event. Driving slowly and arriving on time is always better for your blood pressure.

12. Plan your meals the day before. This will help you set out meats from the freezer or stop at the store, if needed. You can also prepare your lunch for the following day.

13. If you know you will be eating out and you're wanting to eat healthy, plan your order ahead of time. Go for a big salad and water. You won't even need to look at a menu, and you can chat with your friends.

Once you establish routines, they become second-nature, and you can add more valuable and intentional appointments to your day. I love impromptu meals with my boys or a spontaneous ice cream rendezvous. Routines and systems create space for me to add extras, like reading a magazine at my favorite bookstore, visiting a friend, trying out a new farmer's market, researching how to take my job to a new level, or planning an awesome vacation.

QUIET

Remove white noise from your life. Turn the radio off in the car (I mean, except for my radio show). This is such a great time for conversations with your children. Turn the TV off, silence your phone; do whatever you have to do to stop the noise. Silence your phone notifications so as not to be distracted, and check messages at allocated times.

When my boys were little, we had an extremely quiet house — except for that one time one of the boys came home from school with big news. He let me know he had made his own birthday invitations at school and passed them out! I calmly asked, "Well that's awesome son, exactly how many kids did you invite?" He excitedly told me he made copies of the invitation for everyone who attended the entire school. I think we counted around 100 kids came to our house for that little birthday party. Ahhhhh, memories.

Probably one of my favorite seasons was the four years we didn't own a television — and, we didn't die. I have a theory: build a life so wonderful that it's way more fun and exciting than any made-up show you could ever watch on television.

Enjoy This Season

This is your life. You get one shot, don't waste this season. Some seasons may be a little busier than others. Evaluate your schedule and any white noise, and adjust accordingly. Nothing is more important than a peaceful schedule which will, in turn, yield a peaceful life. Do not wish away the season you're in, instead, recalibrate your mind and choose joy and hope during this time in your life. There's no time to stay stuck in the last season. There are too many beautiful todays to create in this season. Stop everything, and find peace in this very day. As you experience peace today, you will have hope for tomorrow — and hope sure looks good on you.

As the seasons of your life change, commit to forward thinking. Commit to growth, and refuse to look back. You learned valuable lessons from your last season which will make future seasons better than ever. My rule: no regrets. I remind myself that I made the best decisions I could make with the information I had at the time. As you pray through every season, you have the confidence that you asked God for help and did all that you could do. The rest was up to Him. Here we are, in this season, asking God for help, reading books to live our best life. We are doing all that we can do and waiting on God for miracles that are on the way. Grandma always said, "Good things come to those who wait."

I remember the season I had two toddlers. I was talking to a friend of mine who had four littles. We were planning a play date, and she was looking at her calendar and said, "Oh, I can't do Thursday. I already have something that day, and I have a rule that we can only have one scheduled event per day."

I responded, "Oh wow! I have a rule too — no more than 25 events in a single day. That's it. I'm very strict about it, too." We laughed, but that day she taught me something. It is okay to spread out the calendar in order to keep the calm in your life. Protect and value every minute of your time with your littles. Before you know it, they will have cars and jobs. No throw-away days. Every day matters, so make each day a good one.

ACTION STEP:

What do you need to add to your calendar to enjoy this season? A weekend getaway? A game night with your family? Maybe you need to select dates for a family vacation or a once-a-week breakfast with each of your children. The most important people in our lives are family. Building and enjoying those relationships is truly living.

Day 9

BUILD A BETTER SCHEDULE

Lack of direction, not lack of time, is the problem.
We all have twenty-four hour days. — Zig Ziglar

Establishing routines and systems in your life will increase flow and maximize productivity. The end result is hope. Build your schedule based on your desired outcomes. Be specific. In order to build an effective daily schedule, establish firm daily routines and create space to work toward your goals.

THE 90-DAY PLAN

Many studies suggest that the sweet spot for hard work intersecting with desired goals is 90 days. Work backward from 90 days, and establish a daily goal that will get you to your

90-day goal. Allot reasonable time in your daily schedule to meet that 90-day goal.

MY DAILY PERSONAL PRIORITIES:

- Time with God
- Connection with my sons (text or phone call)
- Workout
- Radio Show
- Progress toward my current 90-day goal

MY WEEKLY PERSONAL PRIORITIES:

- Connection with my sons: lunch, dinner, or breakfast once a week (or a quick coffee)
- Weekly improvement goals in my job
- Progress toward my 90-day goal

Build your daily schedule based on your priorities. Accomplishing your daily goals will allow you to meet your weekly goals and then your 90-day goals. Deadlines are key. You are hereby officially upgrading your life every 90 days. Way to go! Life is about to get FUN. As you meet specific goals and dreams every 90 days, that leads to peak experiences and a life filled with hope.

THE RULE OF THREE

The Rule of Three, is an effective habit I implemented as soon as I learned about it.[20] Based on teachings from Dr. Benjamin Hardy, a good friend and I created a rule to send one another a text every evening before bed, and state three things we would like to accomplish the following day that would get us closer to achieving our goals. This is not a task list, but rather, a results list. The goal is to complete the list within the next 24 hours. My friend and I laugh because on busy days, it's easy to forget your goals. We have to check our last text message to make sure we are still on target to meet our daily goal. Find a friend to be your accountability partner, someone who will cheer for your wins and help you keep your commitment to yourself.

This Rule of Three habit forces you to create a 24-hour plan. When you wake up in the morning, you already have your to-do list for your day. Creating a list of one to three results-oriented goals in the evening will eliminate decision fatigue in your mornings. Powerful mornings lead to powerful progress.

Never create a to-do list with more than three results for the following day. Creating long lists becomes busy work. A list of three goals becomes intense and focused work. Make the decision to do intentional, meaningful work, as opposed to busy work, and your efforts will result in specific outcomes that will help you meet your goals.

Wayne Gretzky said it best: "You miss one hundred percent of the shots you never take."[21] I have shots I believe God wants me to take. Maybe you can relate. God gives you the desires of your heart. He wants to accomplish great things through you. As you articulate your goals and dreams and take action, you are on the road to accomplish the things God has put on your heart.

As for Wayne's goals, interestingly, his size and strength were considered to be below average for the National Hockey League. He was living proof that if you put passion and hard work into something, you can acquire the title, "Leading Scorer in NHL history." Whatever you want to accomplish, plan for. "I skate to where the puck is going to be, not where it has been."[22] Perfect advice for life, Wayne!

HABITS AND ROUTINES

A habit is defined as a "settled or regular tendency or practice."

A routine is a "sequence of actions regularly followed; a fixed program."

Brushing your teeth before work is a good habit. Making your bed, brushing your teeth, and reading the Bible before work is a good routine. Several good habits done sequentially create a great routine. Routines allow you to effortlessly complete tasks without a lot of decision making. Routines become second-nature and simplify life. As Leonardo da Vinci said, "Simplicity is the ultimate sophistication."

Creating Your Routines

I recently met with a good friend who was overwhelmed by her morning routine. She kept setting her morning alarm earlier to accommodate for everything she needed to get done in her day. After reviewing her week and creating a morning routine and evening routine, she was able to sleep a little later. Changing her morning alarm allowed her to change her bedtime so that she could stay up later with her night-owl hubby. With a few minor adjustments, we rewrote her routines and she was a happy girl. Here are a few tips for managing a busy week and creating routines that bring flow and joy to your life.

1. Write or type out the days of the week across the top of your ROUTINE SCHEDULE.
2. Under each day, create an AM ROUTINE and a PM ROUTINE space.

3. Add all of your fixed appointments in your week to the appropriate day and routine space, AM or PM (Fitness Classes, Church, Early Workdays, Date Night, Family Night, etc.).

4. Create a list of all of your goals for the week, including how many days will be required and how much time is needed on each day.

    Example:

Workout	5 days per week / 30 minutes
Inspiration	7 days per week / 30 minutes
Bible Reading	7 days per week / 30 minutes
Prayer	7 days per week / 30 minutes

5. Add your goals to the days and times that have available space. (Extra space is your time for additional activities and fun.)

6. Adjust your bedtime and morning alarm accordingly. (Recent research concluded that seven hours of sleep resulted in the highest productivity in a day.)

Establishing routines in your mornings, evenings, bedtimes, and weekends will ultimately allow you to effortlessly accomplish your goals. Consistent routines comprised of good habits are the perfect foundation for building a better schedule. You are creating systems which will lead to less decision making and more time to meet spiritual, relational, and financial goals and live a bigger life with little effort. Evaluate your routines every 90 days to ensure you have maximized your days in order to meet your goals.

Proactive Lifestyle

Create the lifestyle you want. Your lifestyle should make you smile and bring peace. If you aren't smiling at the end of the day, it's time to evaluate how you're spending it. When laundry starts piling up or dirty dishes start stacking up, you are creating a reactive lifestyle instead of a proactive lifestyle. Instead of you running your day, your day is running you. It becomes difficult to carry out routines in a timely manner if an undetermined amount of time must be factored in to find misplaced items or you have to clean items before you use them. Routines can easily be carried out when there is order in a home.

Creating a proactive lifestyle is a decision. Proactive means there's a plan in place, a plan to accomplish the goals God has put in your heart. A proactive lifestyle is one where you aren't rushed or overwhelmed because your brain already knows your plan. You have created space for the things that mean the most to you.

We all know the feeling of running late and not being able to find something, keys, phone, shoes, backpack, etc. Losing something in your home and running late sends the whole family into a tailspin. This is not a setup for a good day at school or work. The lack of good habits and routines can actually be quite discouraging and not conducive for creating a hope-filled environment. Start with one new habit at a time, and stack them until old, bad habits are gone. Order in your home will create a peaceful environment and will inspire creativity and hope.

THE TWO-MINUTE RULE

The Two-Minute Rule states that for anything that takes two minutes or less to do, do it now. Don't wait. Don't put it on a list. Do it right away, and you will not have to revisit the task a second time. This will free your mind of miniscule tasks. Get those little things out of the way so that you can pour more energy into the tasks that require more focus and time. When you accomplish tasks quickly, your brain will be motivated to get other tasks done.

FOCUS

Focus on the task at hand without worrying about checking off the next thing on the list. Every goal will be more meaningful as you discipline yourself to engage in and focus on what is in front of you. There is no need to worry about other tasks, because you've made time in your day for what is most important to you. There will be plenty of time to accomplish everything you need to do in the 24 hours you have.

Make the difficult decisions. Decide what to eliminate in your day that is hindering you from priorities. As you commit to focus and intentionality, there will be a calm in your day. You will recognize what is important and what is a distraction. You will see that it's not about finding time; it is all about making the most of your time and building a better schedule. Focus and flourish.

The Sabbath

You will see progress personified when you observe the Sabbath and take a rest. This is crucial. It made the Top 10 list in the Bible (The Ten Commandments). In whatever way you can observe a time of rest, as God has instructed us to do, do so. Observing the Sabbath works similarly to tithing. If you give God 10 percent of your income, God will make your 90 percent go further than if you had kept 100 percent. The same is true with your time. When you give God a Sabbath day, a day of rest, you will accomplish more in your other six days than if you had worked all seven days. Be sure to plan for your Sabbath. Create a day of rest, unplug from work, and enjoy time with the Lord and your family. A great example of God's reward is Chick-fil-A. In 2020, Chick-fil-A, open six days a week, generated $4.3 billion, while KFC, open seven days a week, had sales at $2.27 billion.[23] When you honor God, He honors you. God's plan will allow you to accomplish more in six days than if you had worked all seven. Welcome to God-math, where the numbers do not make any sense to us but always add up to incredible blessings beyond what we could have ever imagined.

VACATIONS

As you are building a better schedule, don't forget the fun. Always include peak experiences, the moments to celebrate the blessings and gifts in your life, in your plan. Schedule vacations by putting them on the family calendar. Whether it's a weekend to visit Grandma, a day trip to a nearby city, or a short getaway, a planned vacation will give you (and the kids) something to look forward to. You can schedule as many getaways as you'd like. There's no rule, you know.

I have a very close friend who set a goal to take six vacations every year. That was three years ago. She made it happen. Planning equals tanning. Just kidding — but that is kind of how that works. My friend and her family have enjoyed everything from beach time to snow skiing. They are making more memories in a year than most people experience in a lifetime. She plans "parents only" trips and family trips. What are you planning? You can start today. And, by the way, some vacations/getaways may cost somewhere in the thousands, but there are lots of options on a budget as well. That's why God made Google. Explore and plan. Make a plan for a family getaway before this year ends! You can do it!

I have a favorite resort that I love to frequent annually, if possible. It isn't far away, but once I check in, I pretend I'm on another continent. I usually let my friends and family know I will be away so my phone is a little quieter. I try not to look at the clock except when I wake up in the morning and when I see the sun setting. It's just a little bit of heaven on earth for me. On my last visit, I stopped by a little shop on the property that I love. The unique home décor and the smell of their spicy-perfumed candles burning while I shop makes my heart happy. One item stood out above all others, a little plaid kitchen towel with two words on it: Live Simply. That oh-so-perfect towel now hangs over the oven door handle in my kitchen, reminding me that sometimes less really is more. I hope you take the time to figure out what may be complicating your life, what extracurricular activities need to go. Say goodbye to busyness and distractions and say hello to peak experiences such as getaways and vacations. Enjoy this season of your life — and, by the way, if you happen to have an extra plane ticket, I'm your girl.

ACTION STEP:

Plan a peak experience. Not kidding. Maybe a date night, a weekend family getaway, or a massage. You may have to cancel something else, but do whatever you have to do to get it on the calendar. Like Grandma used to say, "Well now, that's something to look forward to!"

Day 10

HAPPINESS IS AN INSIDE JOB

*Folks are usually about as happy as they make
their minds up to be. — Abraham Lincoln*

It was laundry day. (I have two sons – I could have started every sentence in this book with those four words.) I was taking clothes out of the washing machine and putting them into the dryer. I was overwhelmed by bills, divorce, parenting, a new job, etc. As I was loading the dryer, I whispered a prayer, "Lord, please help me to find hope. I'm struggling. Please help me, Lord." I'm not exaggerating when I tell you that by the time all of the clothes were loaded into the dryer, I felt a sweet peace in my heart. I felt hope. It actually felt so wonderful it made me smile.

The enemy wants you to feel hopeless. He wants you to give more merit to your feelings than to God's promises. I'm thankful God created emotions and most importantly, the power to manage them. Be aware that the enemy wants you distracted and consumed with your emotions. He wants you so busy analyzing how you "feel," it becomes an all-consuming task to live life on a mountain top with no room for valleys. His plot is to weaken you as you believe there's something wrong with you. He's even helped coin weighty labels that can only be managed by medication. Now, in place of normal emotional responses requiring a time of processing, the enemy wants to dole out permanent labels with no end in sight for treatment. Of course, there are situations that warrant more specific and intense help, but it is important to be self-aware and careful about quick remedies. Never underestimate the value of growth that takes place as you navigate challenges in this life. It's okay to go through seasons of sadness. There is nothing wrong with you feeling sad, hopeless, or anxious, at times. It just means it's time to get alone with God because you are in a serious battle. God is greater, and He's on your side. "The weapons we fight with are not the weapons of the world. On the contrary, they have divine power to demolish strongholds" (2 Corinthians 10:4).

You need to know that you are not alone and there is hope. God has given you tools, and He wants to help you through your challenging seasons. In fact, He doesn't just want you to barely make it through, He wants to take you to victory just like He did with David. In desperation, David pleaded, "Answer me quickly, Lord, my spirit fails. Do not hide your face from me or I will be like those who go down to the pit. Let the morning bring me word of your unfailing love, for I have put my trust in you. Show me the way I should go, for to you I entrust my life" (Ps. 143:7-8). Paul writes in 2 Corinthians 4:8, "We are hard pressed on every side, but not crushed; perplexed, but not in despair."

There will be seasons of pain and suffering. We have a weapon. God's Word will strengthen us and give us hope as we meditate on His promises. God wants to fight for you. He wants to give you hope and a future. We know the plan of the enemy: "The thief comes only to steal and kill and destroy; I have come that they may have life, and have it to the full" (John 10:10). That verse reminds us that the enemy is on a mission. Our job is to recognize when he is at work and call on God to fight for us. A favorite verse I quote in my prayer time often is Exod. 14:14, "The Lord will fight for you; you need only to be still." It reminds me that the battle is the Lord's, not mine. God wants to fight our battles. Call on Him for help. He wants to talk to you. He's waiting at the door. "Behold I stand at the door and knock. If anyone hears my voice and opens the door, I will come in to him and eat with him, and he with me" (Rev. 3:20, ESV).

God sees you right where you are. He understands your pain. He sees your disappointments and heartbreaks. He gets you. A whispered prayer can change everything. God will remind you of verses to strengthen you. "I can do all things through Christ who gives me strength" (Phil. 4:13). The truth of God's Word will override every lie of the enemy. "The Lord is my strength and song; He has given me victory. This is my God, and I will praise Him — my father's God, and I will exalt Him" (Exod. 15:2, NLT). I'm so thankful God gives us His Word to fill us with hope and remind us that He created us to be overcomers. It's our responsibility to be in the Word, hold our ground, and stand strong.

CHECK YOUR HOPE-METER

I'm not trying to oversimplify here, but there is a place for being self-aware and making appropriate adjustments. There are signs to watch for, indicators that you need hope. You may feel helplessness, despair, or depression. These are all warning signs that it's time to take action. This is not the time to allow your thoughts to rule you and allow those negative emotions to fester.

You may laugh, but think of the gauge in Santa's sleigh in the movie "Elf." The more people believed in the Christmas spirit, the more power the sleigh had to fly. (Remember, all they had to do was start singing "loud for all to hear" and the needle would start moving. I'm not sure how it would go if you started singing "loud for all to hear" at work, but don't let me stop you.) We've all been in situations when we've had thoughts like, Oh my, this is a lot. I need to snap out of this. I need to find hope. I have a "Hope Always Wins" list of power moves that I made for myself when I'm feeling low. I give myself a couple of minutes to cry in my coffee or watch a rom-com, and then I get to work on getting control of my emotions.

Set yourself up for a turnaround. If you give Satan an inch, he'll take a mile. Act quickly. These are immediate power moves I make to keep moving in the right direction.

"Hope Always Wins" Checklist:

1. Quote Scripture immediately.
2. Pray through. (Not a quick prayer; I stop everything and talk to God until I feel peace.)
3. Call Mom or a friend for some encouragement.
4. Go for a prayer walk or pray while at the gym.
5. Meet a strong, godly friend for coffee.

6. Clean something (house, car, closet)
7. Buy makeup (kind of kidding, but not really).

There you have it. I've just shared my go-to and get-strong turnaround list. Real life. I acknowledge why I'm sad, and then I start to work on my thoughts, lining them up with God's Word. I make a positive power move. I have a strong conversation with myself that looks something like this, *Um hello, Marla, what are you doing? Are you actually giving Satan the keys to your life? Are you going to let him win? Is God on the throne? Now you're walking in disobedience. This is very serious. Do you trust God to take care of you? Don't you believe Him? You spend most of your days telling people how much God loves them, and does that not apply to you? Hasn't He been there for you every single time? Maybe you should trust Him with this part? Do you have anything you can be thankful for? He's been there all along and He will be again.* I'm not kidding. That is the download convo I have with myself.

If I'm really struggling and I need to hear an encouraging word, I have my go-to list of friends and family I can call. I have people in my life that I know will speak life into me and remind me of God's promises. I have been known to call my close friends and say, "Hey can you help me for a minute? I just need you to remind me that God is hearing my prayers and He has a plan for my life." They are quick to assure me and give me Scriptures to stand on. I listen intently to their powerful words of hope, and then sometimes they will ask if we can pray or I may ask them to pray with me. These are the kind of people you must have in your life. These are my life-line people, my support team. These are the people that do not care about the details. They have no desire to gossip, but only want to lift my arms until I feel strong.

Those same friends call on me for the same reason. They may call me and say, "I'm driving to a meeting and I think something is wrong. Will you pray with me?" I respond, "Of course! Then I tell them Scriptures that come to my mind, such as, "Do not fear, for I am with you; do not be dismayed, for I am your God" (Isaiah 41:10). The Lord is with you. There is supernatural power in God's Word. Make sure you have friends who know God's Word. My friend might say, "I can't thank you enough. I feel good. God is so good. He will take care of this meeting." Friends encouraging friends with strong words of hope — who, together, lean on God for wisdom — that's the power of prayer partners.

Speaking Life or Death

"Death and life are in the power of the tongue, and those who love it will eat its fruits" (Proverbs 18:21, ESV). You are either speaking life and winning or speaking death and losing. If you're spending an inordinate amount of time talking about the battle and your weaknesses, you're speaking death. Don't do it. If you're talking about the hard stuff, you're still losing. Surrender your emotions and ask God what you can learn from this season. Talk about your next move, your comeback, God's faithfulness, miracles in the Bible, miracles in your life, getting on the other side of your challenge, and now you are speaking life. Frame your situation in a way that strengthens you. You can be all alone or you can be in a season of growth and learning. See the difference? The first *you* is a victim, while the other is preparing for a beautiful future filled with hope.

John 10:10 says God wants you to have life and have it to the full. He's reminding you that there is much going on that you can't see. Be patient and let Him work. When you cannot see an end in sight or you cannot imagine a great ending to a current situation, God says, "Do not lose heart." Second Corinthians 4:16-18: "Therefore, we do not lose heart. Though outwardly we are wasting away, yet inwardly we are being renewed day by day. For our light and momentary troubles are achieving for us an eternal glory that far outweighs them all. So, we fix our eyes not on what is seen, but on what is unseen, since what is seen is temporary, but what is unseen is eternal."

When I'm in a battle, and it seems things aren't going as I thought they would, I quote Scripture out loud and I can feel myself getting stronger. God wants to strengthen you in your battle. "For in him dwells all the fullness of the Godhead bodily; and you are complete in him" (Colossians 2:9, NKJV). We are complete in him. We already have all that we need for victory. Be strong and speak faith-filled words.

FINDING THE GOOD

Maybe something traumatic happened that left you wondering how this could be the plan. I still remember the phone call. I was visiting my family in Oklahoma, and my neighbor called to tell me my house was on fire. I couldn't believe it. This was the house where so many teens had come to visit, the house where we were raising our boys. We loved our house. In fact, we were adding on to accommodate more children moving in. I just couldn't believe that anything good could come from this fire.

I drove back to Missouri and saw the devastation. The roof had burned. All of our things stored in the attic were burned up. On the main floor, water and smoke damaged most of our home. I remember fighting back tears and calling my grandma to tell her all about it. Grandma said, "Marla, the Lord will take care of you. He never allows you to lose something without giving you something better in return." I held on to Grandma's words. Thank you, God, for praying Grandmas.

We moved into a temporary place while we figured out where we were going to live. God did a beautiful thing. We found a house, our dream house, all because of that fire. We were forced to leave our little house, and God blessed us with something even better, just as my grandma had said. Maybe you needed to hear those words. Maybe you've lost something or someone and you need a reminder that God is going to take care of you. He loves to bless you beyond anything Satan tries to steal. Keep your faith in God. Your setback is only a setup.

Superheroes

You've seen the superhero movies. You know the ones where the superhero is all suited up and looks strong, handsome (or beautiful), and mighty, and then the enemy shows up. Maybe you're in the part of your movie where you're suited up, and you look and feel great in your superhero outfit. Then the enemy comes. You know the scene, the one where the superhero (you) has to fight the bad guy. There's always that moment when it looks like the enemy might win. You see the superhero lose his balance or sustain an injury. He's holding up his shield while fiery darts and bullets are coming, and the odds are a million to one. And then it happens — the moment we've all been waiting for. The superhero (you) rises from the rubble, finds supernatural strength, and goes on the offense. He has a new strength and conquers the enemy.

God called you to win. Don't get stuck in the middle of the battlefield, lower your shield, and curl up and die. Hold that shield up. The longer you hold it up, the stronger your arms become. Plan your next move. Yes, there are bullets; yes, it's hot in the fire; yes, it doesn't feel good, but what's your next move? Come on, work with me here. The enemy will have to reload at some point, and then you make your move.

What are you doing while you're holding up your shield? Are you getting stronger, are you reading, are you learning, are you seeking God for clarity and open doors? Are you getting inspired to fulfill a calling you have neglected? Do you want to write a book, write a song, lead in your company, go after the promotion, pursue God-inspired goals? Prepare, study, and grow. At reload, you will be prepared, and you will make your move to victory.

DO NOT FEAR

We know where fear comes from. True, the enemy is behind it, but doesn't it come when we disobey God's instructions not to fear? That may be a little harsh, but when I'm afraid, I think of the many times God distinctly tells us not to fear.

Joshua 1:8: "Do not fear and do not be dismayed."
Isaiah 41:10: "Fear not, for I am with you; be not dismayed, for I am your God;"
Isaiah 43:1: "Fear not, for I have redeemed you;"
Jeremiah 46:27: "Fear not, O Jacob my servant, nor be dismayed."
Lamentations 3:57: "You came near when I called on you; you said, 'Do not fear!'"

In fact, "fear not" is mentioned 365 times in the Bible, the exact number of days in the year. There's not one day we should be fearful. When that emotion arises, recognize there's a battle for your thoughts. It's not from God. Pray that feeling away and stand tall. Or you may have to stand tall first and pray until you feel as strong as you appear.

Every morning, God offers the gift of a new start, a new view, and new opportunities. God desires for you to have fervor and zeal that fills your heart to overflowing. He wants you to have joy deep within your soul, a sustaining joy that will make you strong and healthy, inside and out.

You're not alone. God is very clear that "He will never leave you or forsake you" (Heb. 13:5, ESV). He's right there with you. He will comfort you and provide for you. He loves you more than you can imagine. He wants to walk this journey with you — all the way to victory.

What if the journey to victory has a few roadblocks? What if you think you're on the right track and the rug gets pulled out from under you? Then what? Is He still God? Does He still have a plan? Here is where we truly learn to persevere.

Persevere

Persevere, hope in God, stand on His Word, and encourage others even in the midst of your pain. As I was writing this chapter, my phone alerted me of a text, an answer to a prayer I have been praying for several weeks. Thank you for celebrating with me in this moment! You should know, when I started writing this book, I was praying for that miracle, but there was no sign of it. Faith starts writing the book when you don't have your answer. Think about steps you can take in faith today.

As you wait upon the Lord, become a better you. Ask God what He would have you accomplish and work toward in the next 30 days, 6 months, 1 year, 3 years, or 5 years. And, persevere. "Let perseverance finish its work so that you may be mature and complete, not lacking anything" (James 1:4). Pray for God to work in you and give you vision for your future. Pray for strength and courage to walk in obedience, and allow Him to do all He wants to do in you.

You are persevering and not giving up on a miracle. No one else can do that for you. You are building a future committed to God's best and preparing for His awesome blessings in your life. You're getting stronger every day. "Do not grieve, for the joy of the Lord is your strength" (Neh. 8:10). "Do not" seems pretty clear. You have a choice to make. Don't choose grief. Choose joy.

Like you, I'm trusting God for huge miracles in my life. In my personal prayer time, I am making it a habit to praise God. I'm reiterating to the Lord that my answer is YES. Sometimes miracles happen right away, and sometimes God is working many miracles in conjunction with others. We trust His perfect timing. We must persevere and not lose hope. "Not only so, but we also glory in our sufferings, because we know that suffering produces perseverance; perseverance, character; and character, hope" (Rom. 5:3-4).

Hope and trust in God will keep you "turning your mic on" and encouraging others when you have yet to see answers to your own prayers. I love how God works. He gives you an opportunity to stand and speak in faith and then rewards you for your faith. Remember Abraham? "Abraham believed God, and it was credited to him as righteousness" (Rom. 4:3). He was 100 years old, and God told him he would be the father of many nations, yet he didn't have any children. My favorite verse about Abraham is, "Against all hope, Abraham in hope believed and so became the father of many nations, just as it had been said to him, 'So shall your offspring be' .... Yet he did not waver through unbelief regarding the promise of God, but was strengthened in his faith and gave glory to God being fully persuaded that God had power to do what he promised" (Romans 4:18, 20, ESV). What are you praying for? What are you hoping for? Are you fully persuaded, like nothing can change your mind because you know God can do absolutely anything? Did you notice that Abraham began giving God glory because he was so sure that God would fulfill His promise? Whatever you're praying for, start giving God glory.

THE BETTER PLAN

I went through a very public and painful season. A friend of mine called to console me. She started crying and said, "I'm so sorry. Are you sure you're okay, Marla?"

I said, "Yes, I'm good."

"I can't believe how strong you are," she added.

"Here's what I know," I began to explain. "God is so good and so powerful; He will work this for my good. I know it. This just means He has a better plan. How could I cry when He has something better for me? Honestly, I almost feel excited for His plan."

I'm so thankful that God gave me the opportunity to speak life over my situation and increase my friend's faith as she watched me on that journey. As you go through seasons and lean on God for strength, He will use your journey to strengthen others through their challenges.

Trusting God when life doesn't look like you thought it would, is the challenge of all challenges. God knew we would need to be reminded more than once to trust Him. He says it over and over in His Word, which is also why we have to remind ourselves over and over to do it. Taking our thoughts captive is on us. It is our responsibility. "Take every thought captive to obey Christ" (2 Corinthians 10:5, ESV). Long ago, the pastor of my church in Oklahoma, would say, "Pray through." That meant to pray until you feel a supernatural peace. If you're praying for a miracle and you need faith to trust God, pray until you feel strong. Pray until you can smile because you trust the Almighty God of the universe, your Creator, and His great plan for your life. There is absolutely nothing too hard for Him. Pray until you can give Him glory for the miracle that is on the way in your situation. God will intervene. "The Lord's purpose will prevail" (Proverbs 19:21).

As you pray and God infuses you with His supernatural peace and hope, He will give you opportunities to let your light shine. He will bring people on your path who need to hear that there is hope and God loves them. Sharing hope may be a kind word or deed, or it may be a promise to pray for a friend. Inviting someone to church may bring that person the hope he or she has been searching for. God will open doors as you say yes to Him. He will use your voice and your life to give hope to people on your path.

We are no longer victims. Our best days are in front of us, not behind us. Now, we can pray for wisdom and discernment to recognize opportunities that are coming our way to share God's love. We are free from our pasts. You don't live there anymore. The future is way too big to stay stuck in what was.

ACTION STEP:

It's your turn to create your own "HOPE ALWAYS WINS" checklist. This list will keep you from posting possible regrets on social media while you go through your refining fire. Get stronger in the fire. Lean into God. Trust Him with every part of your journey, even this part. Make a list of 7 to 10 power moves you can do right away when you are struggling to find hope. Let's go! We have battles to win.

Day 11

STRONG AND COURAGEOUS

Hope is the companion of power, and mother of success; for who so hopes strongly has within him the gift of miracles. — *Samuel Smiles*

As you get stronger every day, filling your own hope tank, miracles are on the horizon. The miracle of creativity. The miracle of your calling. Miracles that will inspire the world. That's what's on the inside of you when you say NO to fear and YES to hope, YES to being fiercely committed to whatever God has put on your heart.

On-Air

I'm so thankful for my radio show. I have so much fun talking to people on the air and sharing hope. People often ask me if I have a script. The answer is no. I know that God called me to speak life into our listeners, so I pray and ask God for wisdom to know what to say. Before I go on the air, I generally decide on a topic to chat about and then go for it. I feel like it needs to be fresh and conversational, so I don't read a script. I pray and ask God to give me the right words to say, and then I open my mouth. Now, this usually is a wonderful thing, until those little things called bloopers happen. Oh, like the time I went to introduce the awesome Christian artist, Toby Mac, but instead I said, "Coming up next, the amazing TOBY KEITH! OPE! Um, Toby Keith sings alright, but not on our station. He sings on the country one." So, there's that. Then, there was the time I tried to give a traffic report on Sexton Street. That's all I'm going to say about that.

Spreading hope on the radio is my favorite mission. In order to be authentic, I have to keep my emotions in check. Not every day is filled with rainbows and roses, joy unspeakable and full of glory. Some days are challenging. Some days I've just had a hurtful conversation. Some days I still haven't seen the miracle I've prayed for so long to see. Some days I'm waiting on a doctor's report. Just like you, I'm on an imperfect journey, and sometimes it's a rough road.

As long as we stand on the infallible Word of God, we will be strong. It isn't optional. God reminds us to be strong and courageous. When the storm is raging, stand firm on the Word and you will not lose your footing. When the wind is strong and the waves are high, I turn on my microphone and remind my audience, "God is still on the throne, and He has a plan, no matter what it looks like." Give God praise for miracles that are on the way. Have faith, persevere, and watch Him do the impossible.

BEAUTIFUL WORDS

Just like my job is to speak life over the radio, as Christians, God has called us to speak life to those around us. It's not just for the listener. As I speak words of faith and quote God's promises on the radio, I am strengthened myself. Keep your words in check. Think about what you would say if you had a microphone on during every conversation. You have to pray to have the right heart so that your words will speak life. Pretend you are on the radio speaking to a large crowd today. How would you speak life over everyone? What would your words be? "But the things that come out of a person's mouth come from the heart, and these, defile them" (Matt. 15:18). Beautiful words come from a beautiful heart.

You Never Know

I received a call from a listener who said she was sitting in her car crying and feeling so desperate, and I came on the air talking about hope. She said she felt that I was speaking right to her. I had no idea. Then there's John who occasionally calls from prison. He's been there 10 years, and they play our radio station at the facility. He calls me on the studio line when he is struggling to find hope. I share with him the story of Paul and Silas praising God while they were in prison. I pray with him and remind him that God loves him. I encourage him, "Just keep praising God until your situation changes, John."

People need hope. You have no idea who is watching you and being inspired by your life. People want to know that everything is going to be okay. They want to make sure they are not forgotten. God has called us to share His hope with the world. We get to be the ones shouting on the hill, "God still loves you! He still has a plan!"

I'm so thankful that I had parents who raised me to know that I could call on Jesus in my time of need and He would help me. My prayer was to raise my sons the same way. One of my favorite stories of my son sharing hope happened when he was about 14. He and several friends from school were in an elevator. Long story short, the elevator got stuck between floors and the kids were trapped. The story goes that, at first, they thought it was kind of funny and were making jokes. After an hour, it wasn't funny anymore, and the laughter turned to tears. A few of the girls began to cry. There was still no sign of help. Everyone was starting to panic. They said that at one point, my son said, "Hold on, we just need to pray." They said they stopped crying, and my son prayed over their situation. It wasn't long until the fire department arrived and was able to pry the doors open and let a ladder down so the kids could be pulled up to the next floor to safety.

Several of the kids told me the story later. They told me how they were so frightened, and it was in that moment that my son gave them hope. I love that my boy knew who to call on in their time of need. I am so thankful God answered their prayers that day. Hope is a powerful emotion. Hope changes everything. That day, my son showed it to be true that the one who hopes, leads.

Just like in that elevator, we live in a world full of people looking for hope. They are metaphorically trapped in an elevator, and they just need someone to say, "Wait a minute, I know who can help!" They need hope that God will rescue them. They need to know that they will be pulled to safety. This is our cue. We must be the ones to say, "I can't get us out of the elevator, but I know who can." People need our hope. This is our moment to be strong. We may even be in the elevator, too, just like my son, but we know who can help, so we lead the way. We lead by inviting people to church. We lead by sharing God's hope, and then watch Him rescue. What a privilege and responsibility to lead in hope.

SEVEN TIMES HOTTER

How about those three men who stood strong for God, Shadrach, Meshach, and Abednego (Dan. 3)? They were faithful men who showed us how to stand for God and trust Him when we have no idea how it's all going to go. King Nebuchadnezzar was furious when he heard that these men would not bow down to the golden image he created. He had the men brought before him and warned them they would be thrown into the fiery furnace. "Then what god will be able to rescue you from my hand" (Dan. 3:15)?

Those three men were superheroes. When Nebuchadnezzar spoke, how did they respond? "We do not need to defend ourselves before you in this matter. If we are thrown into the blazing furnace, the God we serve is able to deliver us from it, and He will deliver us from Your Majesty's hand. But even if He does not, we want you to know, Your Majesty, that we will not serve your gods or worship the image of gold you have set up" (Dan. 3:16-18). They trusted God whether they lived or died because they trusted the plan they could not see. Are you trusting God with a plan you cannot see? The plan that you have no idea how it's going to play out? Are you strong and resolute that God is still God, no matter the outcome? Be strong. Be resolved that you will trust God no matter what.

Can you imagine knowing that you are going to be thrown into a fire, and then you hear the King announce he wants the fire "turned up seven times hotter than usual?" What? Has your life gotten complicated, maybe seven times more complicated than ever? Stand strong. Trust God's plan, even when the heat is turned up — especially when the heat is turned up. God's about to show up.

Nebuchadnezzar even went as far as ordering his strongest men in the land to throw Shadrach, Meshach, and Abednego into the fire. The fire was so hot it killed the men who threw them in. Maybe Satan has brought in the "big guns." Maybe he's ordered his top guys to take you down. God is bigger than Satan's best. Keep your head, keep your focus, and stay close to God. He will deliver you.

When you're going through a trial, don't put God in a box. He's going to answer your prayer, but it may look a little different than you thought. Maybe you're praying to avoid the fire altogether? That's not how it went for these guys. They didn't avoid the fire. No matter how much they loved and trusted God, they were still thrown into the fire. You may feel like you've been thrown into the fire. Now more than ever, this is an opportunity for God to be God. He is in that fire with you.

Do you see how powerful God is in this story? He gave us details to show just how protective He is of us. Daniel 3 says that those three men came out and didn't even "smell like smoke!" "Not one hair on their head was singed." Stand strong in that fire. You don't have to be a victim of the fire. God can protect you right in the middle of the flames. He will protect your heart and mind. He will make you stronger when you come out. He will make sure not even a hair on your head is singed. He will make sure you don't even smell like smoke. The sooner you release all of the ways you thought it should have gone or will go, the quicker you will sense God's peace even in the midst of your inferno.

There is so much more going on than you can see. So many more people involved than you realize. Let God be God, and rest in His bigger plan. Allow God to use your story to rescue and give hope to many people.

JOSHUA'S KIND OF COURAGE

"Be strong and courageous. Do not be afraid; do not be discouraged, for the Lord your God will be with you wherever you go" (Josh. 1:9). This verse reminds us to take the next step. Be bold. God is with us.

Joshua was taking the lead now that Moses had died. God promised him success, but Joshua had to believe it. "No one will be able to stand against you all the days of your life. As I was with Moses, so shall I be with you; I will never leave you nor forsake you" (Josh. 1:5). It's time to be brave. It's time to believe God. There's a calling on your life. Fear of failing isn't an option. God will help you. If things don't work out like you thought, follow God's lead. Your idea wasn't the best idea. God has a better one.

Someone asked me once, "Aren't you afraid of going on the air and making a mistake?" I always answer, "No. If I make a mistake, I try to learn, forgive myself, and do better the next time I'm on the air." It's a live show, so I do my best "as unto the Lord." The odds of making a mistake are pretty high when you talk on the air as many hours per day as I do. I keep in mind, it's not about me. I correct myself, get better, and move on. If a mistake slows me down, or worse, stops me, the enemy wins. And to that I say, "No way, not today, not on my watch." My prayer is, "Here am I, Lord, send me," and I keep on keepin' on. Do it afraid. One thing I've noticed about myself, the more I do, even when I'm afraid, the less I'm afraid, and the more I do. Don't let the enemy keep you from the blessing waiting on the other side of your obedience.

SHUNAMITE STRONG

Her name is never mentioned in the Bible, but the Shunamite woman's story is one of the most impactful in my life. This woman's story strengthens me. Her faith and courage during her darkest moment inspires me. She was strong. She kept her head. She knew what to do.

The prophet, Elisha, came through town regularly and would stay with the Shunamite woman and her husband. He was so grateful for her kindness. He asked the servant, Gehazi, what he could do for her. Gehazi mentioned that her husband was old and she had no son. Elisha called for her. As she stood in the doorway, Elisha told her, "At this season next year you shall embrace a son" (2 Kings 4:8-17).

She responded, "No, my lord, O man of God, do not mislead your maidservant." It was almost too good to be true. A baby boy! Can you imagine being torn between being excited and, ummmm, how in the world will this happen? The next season came, and guess who got a baby shower? I love that so much. And then, the story takes a terrible turn.

The son of the Shunamite woman was out in the field with his dad, when he shouted out, "Oh my head, my head!" The servant carried the boy to his mom. She held her precious son, her gift from God, and then he died in her arms. She took him upstairs and laid him on the bed, the bed she had put into her house just for Elisha. She called to her husband in the field to bring her a servant and a donkey because she needed to go quickly to find Elisha.

Her husband was baffled and said, "Why are you going today?"

She answered, "All is well." She saddled the donkey, and she and the servant went to find Elisha.

When Elisha saw her coming, he sent his servant out to greet her, "Is all well with you? Your husband? Your child?"

She answered, "All is well." Then, Elisha saw she was in distress. He went to the house and asked God to heal the boy, and the child came back to life.

This woman just had her son die in her arms. She was asked twice, "Is everything okay?" HER SON WAS DEAD. She never wavered once from her answer, "All is well." I have been strengthened so many times by this woman. No matter what it looks like, because I trust God, all is well. That mama spoke hope. She spoke about things that were not as though they were. That's the kind of faith that moves mountains and moves the hand of God. All is well, because we serve the most amazing, merciful, kind, loving, and generous God. When someone asks how I'm doing, you may hear me respond, "All is well." It doesn't mean I have a perfect life; it means I trust my life to a perfect God.

A GOOD REPORT

What are you reporting about your life? What are you seeing? Giants or opportunity? Remember the 12 spies who were sent to the promise land? Ten men came back grumbling that it looked impossible. Two men came back with an enthusiastic report: "Then Caleb silenced the people before Moses and said, 'We should go up and take possession of the land, for we can certainly do it'" (Num. 13:30). Caleb had hope and was brave enough to share it. Then came Joshua's report.

> Joshua son of Nun and Caleb son of Jephunneh, who were among those who had explored the land, tore their clothes and said to the entire Israelite assembly, "The land we passed through and explored is exceedingly good. If the LORD is pleased with us, He will lead us into that land, a land flowing with milk and honey, and will give it to us. Only do not rebel against the LORD. And do not be afraid of the people of the land, because we will devour them. Their protection is gone, but the LORD is with us. Do not be afraid of them" (Num. 14:6-9).

Two men gave the report, God will help us and we will win. They spoke enthusiastically in faith. What did God think of their enthusiastic hope and faith? "But because my servant Caleb has a different spirit and follows me wholeheartedly, I will bring him into the land he went to, and his descendants will inherit it." God not only blessed him for his attitude, he blessed his kids and his kids' kids. In verse 30, he went on to say, "Not one of you will enter the promised land, except Caleb and Joshua," the only two with enthusiastic reports. There's blessing on the other side of enthusiasm. Your words of victory and trust in God, when things look impossible, bless God. In turn, He will bless you. Stand strong. Believe in God's ability and willingness to do incredible things in your life and your children's lives. Blessing follows wholehearted faith.

Faith

Faith is a must if you want to please God. Be so full of faith you actually cause others to have faith. "And without faith it is impossible to please God, because anyone who comes to him must believe that he exists and that he rewards those who earnestly seek him" (Heb. 11:6). As you are pleasing God with your faith, start watching. He promised rewards. Your life is about to get awesome!

ESTHER 2:1-23

Remember Esther's rise from poverty to a palace? She was an orphan being raised by an older cousin (Mordecai). He loved Esther and took good care of her, but what part of her story would cause us to believe that one day she would be a queen? That's how God works. He loves a good plot twist. As you're reading this book, I'd like to suggest that you prepare for one of those in your life. Not kidding.

Maybe, metaphorically speaking, you're in the part of your story where you've just been orphaned. Maybe you are tired and nothing seems to be happening, and you're struggling to find hope. Maybe you can't seem to catch a break lately. Hold on. It's not over. You have a few decisions to make in order to prepare for your palace.

When the king was looking for a queen, all of the women were summoned to the palace. They were given the opportunity to adorn themselves with whatever they desired from the women's quarters before they were brought in to see the king. But when it was Esther's turn, she "requested nothing but what Hegai the king's eunuch, the custodian of the women, advised" (v. 15). God took care of this orphaned girl. He gave her a new story. "Esther obtained favor in the sight of all who saw her," and the king "loved Esther more than all of the other women, and she obtained grace and favor in his sight more than all the virgins; so, he set the royal crown upon her head and made her queen" (v. 17). Did you notice that as Esther attended to what was right in front of her, God took care of everything else? Oh, and then, she saved a nation.

Your amazing story is unfolding and it's a beautiful story — a story of victory, a story of passion, a story of peace, a story of growth. You are writing this story. Make sure it's a good one. "The heart of man plans his way, but the Lord establishes his steps" (Prov. 16:9, ESV). As you plan the course of your life, hold onto your plans loosely. God will put your steps in the right order. We do all that is within our power and responsibility to do, and watch God supernaturally and exponentially multiply the results.

ACTION STEP:

For what area of your life do you need to give a good report? If you are up against a battle of giants, be unstoppable. Speak victorious words like Caleb, "I certainly can do it!" Stop, say a prayer and stand mightily on God's Promises. NOTHING is impossible with God. And, NOTHING means NOTHING. Choose powerful thoughts and powerful words over your giants! Prepare for victory!

$\mathcal{D}$ay 12

ENTHUSIASM IS CONTAGIOUS

Nothing great was ever achieved without enthusiasm.
— Ralph Waldo Emerson

Enthusiasm (noun): Intense and eager enjoyment, interest, or approval.

This beautiful life! What an awesome adventure with twists and turns I never could have anticipated. As I look back, I cannot think of a single boring day. My past has been filled with incredible joy and intense pain. My future won't be boring either. It is sprinkled with plans for fun and connection. I have hope because I have the truth of Jeremiah 29:11, "For I know the plans I have for you, declares the Lord, plans to prosper you and not to harm you, plans to give you hope and a future." I stand on this verse to remind me of the truth, that amazing, prosperous days are ahead.

Life is as exciting and adventurous as you want it to be (at every age, I might add). An adventure involves an unusual and exciting experience. Think of life this way, make it unusual and exciting. An adventure usually calls for exploring unknown territory. If that doesn't describe this life, I don't know what does. We have no idea what tomorrow holds. How exciting to explore the unknown!

How are you describing your adventure? If I see you at the store and ask, "Hey! How are you?" how do you respond? Do you say, "Well, if you really wanna know" or "Don't ask" or "I've been better" or "I'm fine"? This is really important. We need to think about our answers to this question. Take a minute and decide, starting now, how you will answer this question. Choose a powerfully positive answer that speaks life over you. "I'm great! I'm excited to see a couple of miracles happen soon. I'm looking forward to all that God has in store for this day!" You see where I'm going with this. Your words direct your life. Don't take that lightly.

WORRY

Beware of the enthusiasm stealer — worry. God addresses this. It feels like a million pounds have been lifted off my shoulders when I remind myself that God doesn't instruct us to figure anything out. In fact, the Bible repeatedly reminds us to trust in the Lord and do not fear. According to Merriam-Webster, worry (verb) is "to give way to anxiety or unease; allowing one's mind to dwell on difficulty or troubles." I find it interesting that the dictionary clearly points to a choice being made. "Give way" and "allowing" are both referring to a decision that is in our hands to make, thoughts we can choose. In order to stop worry, we have to override those negative thoughts, replacing them with Scripture and truth. One of the Scriptures I decided had to be a go-to Scripture for my life is, "Finally, brothers, whatever is true, whatever is honorable, whatever is just, whatever is pure, whatever is lovely, whatever is commendable, if there is any excellence, if there is anything worthy of praise, think about these things" (Phil. 4:8). There is a battle going on for your thoughts. My most challenging times are when I'm vacuuming or washing my car. Anything that doesn't require a lot of concentration is an opportunity for negativity. My battle-winning verse, Philippians 4:8, gives me a standard to measure my thoughts against. That verse holds me accountable for my thoughts. Do they line up with God's instructions? Am I walking in obedience?

What about trusting God with the people on your journey? Maybe you've been through divorce, or a parent left, or a best friend turned on you, or someone wrote you off.

What if all of that was for your good? What if it looked like rejection, but that person wasn't supposed to be part of your future? No one's absence can keep you from the plan God has for you. What if as long as that person was in your life, you could not have gotten to the place God wanted to take you? Years ago, I felt so sad about a situation in my life, and a friend looked at me and said, "The gift of goodbye."

Here is a good little story I once read:

> My mama told me she walked in on a couple of friends talking about her and they didn't know she was in the room, and she smiled and walked away. My mother also told me she had another friend that talked about her and she knew, and she never mentioned it, and she laughed about it. So, I asked my mama, why do you laugh when you know your friends betrayed you? She said every time she comes to a crossroad and she has to decide who is going on the next journey with her, God shows her the ones that can't come. So, she said never get mad at a person that you called friend, if they betray you. Gracefully bow out and enjoy the new journey with the new people God will put on your new journey.

CONFIDENCE

"I can do all things through Him who strengthens me" (Phil. 4:13, ESV). God promises that you can do all things because of His strength, not your own. As you are confident God is working on your behalf, you can be enthusiastic about your future. The enemy will attempt to discourage you and attack your confidence. He will cause you to doubt that God is at work and question His ability to make absolutely anything possible. Your weapon to put the enemy in his place is Scripture. God's Word is greater than any attack of the enemy. You are guaranteed success. When doubt and fear try to take over, Scripture will strengthen you. You have all the tools you need to hold your head high and watch God fight your battle.

"But those who hope in the Lord will renew their strength. They will soar on wings like eagles; they will run and not grow weary; they will walk and not be faint" (Isaiah 40:31). Are you ready to win your battle? It is a choice to hope in the Lord and watch Him renew your strength. Every day you will get a little stronger than the day before. The more solitary time you spend with God, the faster you will move to the next level of your life. You get to decide. If you've been stuck, hope wants to pull you out of the mire. The minute you picked up this book, you connected to hope. If you will keep your foot off the brake, hope will pull you right out of the trenches, and you can hit the gas and get where you want to go.

POWER

Enthusiasm is power. No one wants to follow a discouraging leader, but everyone wants to follow an enthusiastic one. Just as a magnet attracts metal, enthusiasm attracts followers. An incredible blessing and a great responsibility, enthusiasm carries much power. Enthusiasm will transform your life and the lives of every person on your path. Enthusiasm infuses hope.

I followed the Lord's leading and enthusiasm and wrote this book. Every day I woke up with an insatiable desire to share hope. I practically ran to my computer every chance I got. By the way, when you have a decision to make and you aren't sure what to do, my pastor, John Lindell, always advises, "Let peace and enthusiasm be your umpire." I had such a peace and excitement. I knew I was doing exactly what God asked of me. I had never even wanted to write a book before now. I knew that only God could have put this desire in my heart. You, my friend, are holding a miracle. I'm not sure if it's a miracle for me or for you or for both of us, but I love to watch God orchestrate the details of our lives. Hang tight; you're next!

You Have Everything You Need

What gets you up in the morning: work, school, cooking, creating? What incredible goals are you going after? You can start with something simple; accomplish that little goal and celebrate. Then, move on to something bigger. Think outside of the box. What goals would you set if you knew you really could accomplish them? What dream would you go after if failure was not an option? What if this time next year you would be exactly where you want to be and doing what you feel called to do? Remember, you will never go anywhere that you haven't first envisioned in your mind.

As you are seeking the Lord in prayer and reading His Word, He will give you clarity. He will confirm your goal. "My sheep listen to my voice; I know them, and they follow me" (John 10:27). You may have something in your heart that immediately comes to mind when I talk about your next adventure or goal. Maybe you need hope to believe that you can accomplish it. The fact that you're holding a book written by me — well — that should inspire you to run after any and every goal or dream you've ever had. If I can do it, so can you. If you need confirmation, please let this book be that for you. "Take delight in the Lord, and he will give you the desires of your heart" (Psalm 37:4). Follow His lead. He will never steer you wrong. Your goal may be the next awesome miracle on this planet. Your next move may be the most powerful action step you can take to get you right where God wants you. Walk in obedience, and watch God take the lead.

You can be excited and hope-filled about your future because God promises good things to those who seek Him and wait, and He cannot lie. Have you done all that you can do with what is right in front of you? Have you made the most of every opportunity God has put in your path? Stay alert. The enemy will present distractions to keep you too busy to follow God's plan. Stay close to God, and He will give you the insight to know the difference between opportunity and distraction.

CELEBRATE

Make sure you have people in your life who will celebrate your victories with you, friends who will cheer for you. Surround yourself with encouraging and supportive people. It's important to celebrate victories. Carefully select your support team. Pray for God to give you at least five amazing people who inspire and celebrate you. Share your miracles with one another. Inspire one another. Your good news may encourage someone not to give up and to hope again for their miracle. "Therefore encourage one another and build each other up" (1 Thess. 5:11). Find those people. Be that person.

Celebrate God's favor. He will give you favor at work. He will give you favor in your community. He will give you favor in your relationships. Work hard at what is right in front of you and celebrate your wins. I'm talking about the blessings and opportunities God has entrusted you with today. Give your best to the people around you, your job, and your church. Celebrate your accomplishments at your work and in your relationships. Celebrate God's love for you. You don't have to lose sleep wondering if He still loves you or if He's left you. He does love you, and He's right there. Celebrate miracles on the way, He will deliver. He will provide all that you need, exactly when you need it. Faith celebrates *before* you see the victory.

CAREER CHANGES

Decades ago, a good friend came over to my house. She asked me to pray with her about a big decision she needed to make regarding her career. She had always been in restaurant management, but she was about to buy her own restaurant. That was scary. We sought the Lord together for wisdom for her journey. I prayed for her often. She went for it. Years later, her business ended up being both of my sons' first jobs when they were old enough to work. Not too long ago, she took me for a ride in her airplane. God is so good. Invest in others and watch Him bless you too.

Maybe you've experienced a scary career change or you're in the middle of one. Trust God. I have found that when I've done all God has told me to do, I can trust Him with the changes. Leaving a job may mean leaving a comfort zone. Trust God. Don't hold onto something just because that is all you have ever known and it's familiar. God may want to do something new in your life. He may want to take you in a new direction. Trust Him in the process. Follow His lead as He opens and closes the doors that are a crucial part of your next move. He's pretty good at that stuff.

I had a wonderful job in Branson, Missouri. I thought I would work there forever. I worked with some friends of mine at their company, employing hundreds of people. I loved that job. One day, the company board decided to go a different direction with my department. I was devastated. I couldn't think of one way this was going to work for my good. And then, it all changed. God opened a door that made my last job look boring. God loves to surprise us! By the way, that company doesn't exist today. I didn't know it at the time, but God saved me. What I thought was a devastating blow was a rescue. God took me in a new direction months before the whole operation would shut down. Trust Him, no matter what it looks like.

OPPORTUNITY

God will show you opportunity. He will open doors for you to spread hope to those on your path. I just sat down to finish writing this chapter. This is so incredible you're going to think I made it up. You see the first two sentences of this paragraph? That is the last thing I typed before I left for work this morning. Those two lines are all I had written, and I headed off to work.

After I got to work, I started my show. After the first break, I took my headphones off and saw something out of the corner of my eye, outside my studio window. I couldn't figure out what it was, so I went to the window to get a closer look. That's when I saw, leaning against the brick column, a person sitting on the ground with a hoodie over her head, holding her knees to stay warm.

I walked outside, and as I got closer, I could see it was a frail young girl, and she was crying. I knelt down beside her and I said, "Hi. Are you okay?"

She looked up at me with teary blue eyes and said, "Yeah, I'm okay."

I asked where she lived and how she got here. I could see by the mascara on her hoodie sleeves that she had been crying for a while. She had the sweetest eyes. Every time I would speak hope to her, she would light up and look me in the eyes as if to say, "You promise?" I reminded her that everything was going to be okay because God loves her. I asked her if she had asked God for help and reminded her that He loves to help us.

She said, "No, I haven't asked in a long time. I guess I should do that." I told her that God was going to help her. Then, I told her that I needed to run inside for a minute to do my work and I'd be right back.

I went back inside the station, and I was trying to find food for her. I looked everywhere and then I went to one of my coworkers, "By any chance, do you have any food for a hungry young girl outside?" Liz looked at me and then grabbed a package of unopened crackers and a little jar of peanut butter. I said, "Oh thank you!"

I wish you could have seen that young girl's face when I walked up with crackers and peanut butter. She was so hungry and so happy. In order to keep this book G-rated, I'll just say her response was the equivalent of, "Oh, heck yeah!"

It was time for me to go back on the air, so I had to run in for a minute. Liz met me in the hall and said, "Well, that explains what happened to me in the store the other day. I bought a jar of peanut butter and as I was walking away, I felt like I was supposed to buy two. Now I know."

Another friend at work, had been through an incredibly rough season. I asked her if she would help me and talk to this young girl. She said, "Oh, yes! I'll go talk to her. I've been where she is!" Rebecca went out and encouraged the young girl for some time. They exchanged cell phone numbers and made plans to meet at church the next night. While they were talking, Liz and I found a jacket for her and free coupons for lunch at a restaurant around the corner. Tears came to my eyes as I began to thank God for giving my friends and me the opportunity to speak hope into this young girl's life.

I watched her get up and walk toward the restaurant. I smiled and said to myself, "God is going to do amazing things for her. This is the first day of the rest of her life."

When I say that God will bring people on your path to share hope, prepare for the opportunities that will come your way, maybe even today. He will do exactly that for you. Ask Him to show you. Ask Him for wisdom to know what to say. He will go before you. We are an army on a mission from God to spread hope in this world. It's time to get strong, gear up, and report for duty. As you take time to help someone find hope again and encourage them to follow his or her calling, God will provide all that you need to follow yours. I have seen this over and over in my life. Those setups for you to help someone are really setups for your own life. God wants to take you to a new place. He's bringing you the opportunity to help someone else so He can show you His favor and bless you.

The Smile

I remember a time in my life when I felt alone. I had to give myself a pep talk just to go to the store. The most important person to encourage and infuse hope into is you. You talk to yourself more than anyone else in the whole wide world. Speak words of hope, compassion, and love over yourself. Don't forget to give yourself pep talks filled with God's promises. Remind yourself to be strong. Remind yourself that if you believe God, you can smile because you trust His Word. You can have joy on the journey. You can correct yourself and remind yourself to straighten up and not lose your passion. "Never be lacking in zeal, but keep your spiritual fervor, serving the Lord. Be joyful in hope, patient in affliction, faithful in prayer" (Rom. 12:11-12).

One particular day, I was sitting in my car, about to go into the store, and I whispered one little prayer, "Lord, could you send someone my way, in this store today, that will smile at me, and I will know everything is going to be alright?" I got out of the car, grabbed my cart, and started walking down the aisles. I was trying to think of what I needed to buy. Nothing sounded good. I got to the end of the first aisle, and as I was going around the endcap, a cart was coming down that aisle toward me. I still remember her face. She was probably in her forties. She had the sweetest round face and gold-rimmed glasses. I started to look at the shelves, but there was a moment when this lady stopped and looked at me with the kindest eyes I had ever seen and smiled so intentionally, I felt like she was an angel. I smiled back and kept walking. I felt tears well up in my eyes and thanked God for her smile that I knew came from Him.

Some days you may need a smile, and some days you may be the one to give the smile. God will show you His love for you. He always surprises me when I ask Him for help. He shows me in some small way how much He loves me; I just have to look for it. Don't miss an opportunity to be the lady in the store who brings the encouragement. We all have a role to play. I pray that as God strengthens you on your journey, you will be enthusiastic about your incredible future. Watch for God to open doors for you to share your story and spread joy. There are people in your life who desperately need to know that God is a whisper away and He will meet their needs. It's a beautiful day to be enthusiastic for Jesus.

ACTION STEP:

Do you need to step up your enthusiasm game? Ask God to help you have an enthusiastic energy and share it with the people in your life! Don't let a day go by without being enthusiastic about all that God is doing in your life and in the lives of the people around you. Celebrate!

Day 13

GIVING

Remember this: Whoever sows sparingly will also reap sparingly, and whoever sows generously will also reap generously. — 2 Corinthians 9:6

"Give, and it will be given to you. A good measure, pressed down, shaken together and running over, will be poured into your lap. For with the measure you use, it will be measured to you" (Luke 6:38). I love how God asks us to give and then blesses us more than we could ever imagine. One such instance happened right in front of my eyes.

It all started when I was playing with my sons in the yard. We had a little cherry tomato garden, and every day we'd see how many tomatoes had ripened since the day before. My then four-year-old would eat them as fast as we picked them, while my then two-year-old was more interested in his swing set. We were always outside. We lived in a neighborhood that had lots of kids who lived close-by and they loved my sweet boys.

The school bus would come by in the afternoon and a couple of kids would get off and come talk to the boys and me. That went on for a week or so, and then I noticed more and more kids getting off at the bus stop by our house. It wasn't long until I counted 16 teenagers hanging out in the yard. I started going to the store and looking for snacks for all of these kids. We didn't have a lot of money, so when I found those little flavored popsicle packets, I thought I had hit the jackpot. Every day I would serve the kids those popsicles and talk to them about their day. I told some friends of mine, "It's like they just want someone to talk to, someone to listen to them." It soon became a highlight in my day.

I noticed over time, listening to their stories, that many of them had parents who were in jail or they lived in single-parent homes and their parents were working a lot of hours. I would talk to the kids about how much God loved them. We would laugh together, cry together, and pray together.

I remember my sister-in-law coming by and seeing all of the kids. I looked at her and said, "I'm not quite sure what to do with all of them."

She said, "Why don't you take them to church?" Best idea ever.

We would fill our car with kids and head to church on Sundays and Wednesdays. After a week or two, we didn't all fit in the car anymore. Some kids would take their cars and we would have a convoy heading to church. Kids were getting saved, and their lives were changing right before our eyes. God was giving them hope. It was a wonderful season to be a part of.

We all became like a big family — a family of 62 to be exact. The kids didn't always come all at once, but we usually had around 30 at the house at a time. I would get phone calls all hours of the day and night. One boy, in particular, would call when he was scared or if his mom didn't come home that night. It was an honor and privilege to love these kids like they were my own. I had always wanted lots of kids when I was growing up, and God answered my prayer.

The kids started asking me to come have lunch with them at school, so I did. I would sit at their table and talk to them about Jesus and invite their friends to church. The school had a policy that you could only eat with the kids if you were family or clergy. Somehow, word got around town about all that was happening at my house, and teachers began to come to the lunch table and thank me. The next thing I knew, I was invited to parent/teacher conferences and school programs galore. God was doing amazing things in all of our lives.

People in the community were so supportive. I called a dentist friend and asked for a favor. One of the kids had an abscessed tooth that was swelling rapidly. The dentist said, "Bring him in. Swelling like that can go to the brain too quickly. Come by tomorrow morning." He got my boy (I called him mine) in that day, pulled the tooth, and didn't charge me. God took care of us. Over and over, we would see the hand of God move in impossible situations and work miracles in all of our lives.

Eventually, the only way we could get all of the kids to church was to rent a bus. Aaaaand then we needed to hire a driver. The more our family did for the kids, the more God provided for all of our personal needs. The kids watched God provide. They saw Him take care of all of us as we stayed close to Him. God moved in miraculous ways in the lives of our little, I mean, gargantuan family.

As Christmas was around the corner, I wondered what we would be able to do for all of the kids. Several of them were at the house one evening and the doorbell rang. I opened the door to see a friend of mine who had heard about the number of kids that were coming over regularly. She handed me buckets of fried chicken, and bags of sides, and a check. She said, "I'd just like to bless your kids for Christmas." I looked down and it was a check for $1,000. It was so wonderful to see the kids' faces as they watched God continually bless our "family."

The grocery bill kept getting bigger and bigger, so we prayed harder and harder. I was checking out at the store one Friday, and the clerk told me the amount was $415 and some change. I knew the food that I was buying would last for about a week or two. I thought maybe I misunderstood. I looked at her, and she repeated the amount. I looked down at my checkbook and began to write. As I wrote out the amount, I whispered under my breath, "As unto you, Lord. I know you will take care of all of our needs." God gave me peace and faith to trust Him to provide.

No matter how many kids came to our house or how many days they stayed, we always had enough food. It was just like the fishes and loaves Bible story. God would always multiply our food. No matter how many kids joined us for dinner, there were always leftovers.

About two weeks went by, and one day my husband came home and said, "You won't believe what happened today." He had purchased a domain name that was one of the most brilliant names of all internet domain names. On this particular day, someone contacted him and made a very generous offer to purchase that name. He agreed and sold it for $250,000. That's right — a quarter of a million dollars. I think that covered the cost of all those Kool-Aid packs and then some. Only God.

CHILDREN ARE A BLESSING FROM GOD

God did a beautiful thing. That season of my life with those 62 children was many years ago. I still talk to several of those kids, although they aren't kids anymore. Most of them are in their 30s and 40s. Many of them got married and had babies. I could not be any prouder of those kids. One of the boys grew up to have many children and has excelled in his job, being in management for years (the only one in his family to work his way up in a company). One of the girls grew up to be an incredible occupational therapist. She's married and has two amazing children, and we still attend the same church, the one where she gave her heart to Jesus. Over the years, I have been invited to attend the births of a number of their children. I've shared amazing moments with those kids. I thank God over and over that I was able to play a small role in such a beautiful plan, in a season when I had no idea how it would all play out.

"Let us not grow weary in doing good, for at the proper time we will reap a harvest if we do not give up" (Galatians 6:9). There are some things that are out of our control and some things that are completely and solely in our control. Our focus must be to do everything with excellence. There are opportunities for you to plant seeds and pour into what is right in front of you. You will reap a harvest in due season. Do good. Where can you plant seeds of goodness? Are you volunteering and pouring into others? Are you planting seeds that will yield a bountiful crop when the time is right? Tithing, encouragement, kindness, gentleness, time, and love are all seeds you want to plant. They will yield an incredible harvest and future.

A Triple Blessing

During the season I was blessed to be a school teacher, God did a pretty wonderful thing. I'm not telling this story because of what I did. I want you to see that it was nothing compared to what God did. I enjoyed doing life with my sweet students and their families.

I remember a mom coming to me after school one day, as she was struggling financially. She had five children and couldn't pay her bills. I just so happened to be saving up money for a family vacation, and I had $500 cash in a shoe in my closet. I had plans to buy plane tickets and surprise my family. The thought crossed my mind, *If I give this mom the money, I may never see it again.* Then came the nudge that I knew was God wanting me to help her. (It's so humbling when God gives us an opportunity to be part of a miracle.)

I went home and got the money and brought it back to her. She told me she'd pay it back in a week. I was praying in my car and had already decided I was giving it as unto the Lord, and I knew God would take care of us, even if I never saw the money again. One week later, that mom paid the money back to me. Wow, I was so thankful. And then, something pretty cool happened.

A year later that mom happened to marry a multi-millionaire. The first thing she did was come to me to tell me she wanted to bless me. She took me shopping and bought me surprises. She was always buying me clothes. It was blessing after blessing. When I think back, she literally spent thousands of dollars over several years on gifts for my family and me. I'm ALWAYS overwhelmed by God's love and all the ways He loves to surprise us with gifts bigger than we could have ever imagined.

DEVELOPING CHARACTER

The Proverbs 31 woman was a giver. She gave generously of her time and her love. Study the way she gave. Let's be givers like she was. (Single guys, this makes a great checklist of qualities to look for in a future wife.)

For my girlfriends, just a fun little note: she had maidservants (Hey, God can send help.). Do these things. Let's plant the seeds of giving by studying God's Word and becoming the women He has called us to be.

Proverbs 31 - The Woman Who Fears the Lord

[10] An excellent wife who can find? She is far more precious than jewels.

[11] The heart of her husband trusts in her, and he will have no lack of gain.

[12] She does him good, and not harm, all the days of her life.

[13] She seeks wool and flax, and works with willing hands.

[14] She is like the ships of the merchant; she brings her food from afar.

[15] She rises while it is yet night and provides food for her household and portions for her maidens.

[16] She considers a field and buys it; with the fruit of her hands she plants a vineyard.

[17] She dresses herself with strength and makes her arms strong.

[18] She perceives that her merchandise is profitable. Her lamp does not go out at night.

[19] She puts her hands to the distaff, and her hands hold the spindle.

[20] She opens her hand to the poor and reaches out her hands to the needy.

²¹ She is not afraid of snow for her household, for all her household are clothed in scarlet.

²² She makes bed coverings for herself; her clothing is fine linen and purple.

²³ Her husband is known in the gates when he sits among the elders of the land.

²⁴ She makes linen garments and sells them; she delivers sashes to the merchant.

²⁵ Strength and dignity are her clothing, and she laughs at the time to come.

²⁶ She opens her mouth with wisdom, and the teaching of kindness is on her tongue.

²⁷ She looks well to the ways of her household and does not eat the bread of idleness.

²⁸ Her children rise up and call her blessed; her husband also, and he praises her:

²⁹ "Many women have done excellently, but you surpass them all."

³⁰ Charm is deceitful, and beauty is vain, but a woman who fears the LORD is to be praised.

³¹ Give her of the fruit of her hands, and let her works praise her in the gates.

For my guy friends, these wise words from Timothy set a great bar of things to pray for and aspire to. To all the single ladies (don't even hum that song), this makes a great checklist to pray for your future honey.

1 Timothy 3:1-7

It is a trustworthy statement: if any man aspires to the office of overseer, it is a fine work he desires to do. An overseer, then, must be

(1)   above reproach,
(2)   the husband of one wife,
(3)   temperate,
(4)   prudent,
(5)   respectable,
(6)   hospitable,
(7)   able to teach,
(8)   not addicted to wine or
(9)   pugnacious, but
(10) gentle,
(11) peaceable,
(12) free from the love of money.
        He must be one who
(13) manages his own household well, keeping his children under control with all dignity but if a man does not know how to manage his own

household, how will he take care of the church of God, and

(14) not a new convert, so that he will not become conceited and fall into the condemnation incurred by the devil.

(15) And he must have a good reputation with those outside the church, so that he will not fall into reproach and the snare of the devil.

Titus 1:5-9

For this reason, I left you in Crete, that you would set in order what remains and appoint elders in every city as I directed you, namely, if any man is above reproach, the husband of one wife, having children who believe,

(16) not accused of dissipation or

(17) rebellion. For the overseer must be above reproach as God's steward,

(18) not self-willed,

(19) not quick-tempered,
not addicted to wine,
not pugnacious,
not fond of sordid gain, but

hospitable,

(20) loving what is good,

(21) sensible,

(22) just,

(23) devout,

(24) self-controlled,

(25) holding fast the faithful word which is in accordance with the teaching, so that he will be able both to exhort in sound doctrine and to refute those who contradict.

I'm so thankful God doesn't leave it up to us to try and figure out which character traits to develop. He so clearly lines out all of the areas in our lives where we need to grow and become more like Him. As we give God our whole hearts and pray to be all that He desires for us to become, He will grow us. As we stand before God with open hands and open hearts, He will give us opportunities to be givers. He sets us up for blessings! Brian Tracy said, "Always give without remembering and always receive without forgetting."

ACTION STEP:

Where can you plant a seed today? Is there a part of your life where you would like to see a harvest? Plant a seed in someone else's life in the same area you are praying for, and watch God bless your life in that same area. Prepare to reap what you sow. It's the Law of the Harvest — and exactly how God works.

$\mathcal{D}ay$ 19

Big Goals, Big Wins

*Hustle (verb): to take massive action with
the resources at your disposal.*

As you run after God, you will cultivate habits and attitudes that will lead to big wins in your life. It's time to use your resources and take massive action. Hustle and meet your goals. *You can't lean on a shovel and pray for a hole.* Seeds grow on good ground. Do the work to create good soil for a spectacular crop that's coming. "Still other seed fell on good soil, where it produced a crop – a hundred, sixty or thirty times what was sown" (Matt. 13:8).

My father was an incredible example of persevering and going after your dreams. You see, not a whole lot of people knew that my father never graduated high school. He dropped out after tenth grade and got a job. (In his 20s, he went back and got his GED.) His family was poor. His father, my Grandpa Jake, could fix anything on any car, but until his dying day in his 80s, he never learned to read or write.

Daddy and I were talking one day and he said, "Remember, a person may be smart about the things they've studied or their interests, but that doesn't make them smarter than anyone else. They're smart about the things they've studied. Your Grandpa Jake couldn't read or write, but he was one smart mechanic. He knew more about cars than most people. He could fix just about anything on any car. People aren't dumb. They're just smart about different things." My father was a very wise man.

Dad always encouraged me to humbly go after my goals. Whatever I wanted to do, he wanted me to be the best at it. He taught me to think big and remove any thoughts that implied something was too hard or out of reach. Ask God to give you good ideas and goals to accomplish. He cares about your goals. "I will instruct you and teach you in the way you should go; I will counsel you with my eye upon you" (Ps. 32:8). God will give you direction and open doors for you. It's our job to watch for God's opened doors and trust Him as we walk through them. There is a clear path, and when you seek the Lord, He will speak. If we listen, He will lead. God's desire is to lead you. "I am the Lord your God, who teaches you what is best for you, who directs you in the way you should go" (Isa. 48:17).

God will surprise you with opportunities you didn't see coming! If you stop and think about it, hasn't He done that for you so many times? A loving friend helped you through a crisis, someone called you out of the blue just when you needed it most, you got a raise, there was a sale, you saw something in nature that got your attention and made you feel like God Himself was close by, and on and on. Fifty percent of opportunity is recognizing there is an opportunity. Whether it's an opportunity for God to take you to a new level or He's about to take you in a new direction. Pray for open doors and vision to recognize those open doors.

HARD WORK

Born and raised in Oklahoma, working hard was in my DNA. Right after my 16th birthday, I got dressed up and was heading out the door. My dad looked at me, "Well, where are you heading to?"

I replied, "I'm going out to get a job. I'll have one by the end of the day, before I get back." We both smiled. I knew God would bless my initiative. I knew He would take care of me. I had seen it too many times in my life already. I came home later that afternoon, excited about my new job as a sales associate at a local retail store, starting that next Monday. I'm a firm believer that God blesses hard work. "And whatever you do, whether in word or deed, do it all in the name of the Lord Jesus, giving thanks to God the Father through him" (Col. 3:17).

God will honor your hard work. He will provide for you and your family as you walk in obedience and do the work in front of you. We have the opportunity to leave a legacy of the joys and rewards of hard work. "All hard work brings a profit, but mere talk leads only to poverty. The wealth of the wise is their crown, but the folly of fools yields folly" (Prov. 14:23-24).

TEAM

Your success depends significantly on who you are surrounding yourself with. Who's on your team? Who are your friends? Who are your encouragers? Who are your challengers? Be particular. Choose people who want you to win, and challenge you to keep growing. These people are your resources, your support. They will add value to your life through their love, encouragement, knowledge and experience. Your team may even consist of people you don't know personally, like authors or preachers. Or, your team may be family members, close friends, co-workers, or your church family. Choose people who inspire and challenge you. Choose people whose standard is the Bible and who serve the Lord wholeheartedly, people who walk in obedience to God's Word. Dr. Benjamin Hardy is on my team. I don't know him personally, but I listen to his wise counsel regarding living an inspired life, and I appreciate his heart for teaching God's Word. I love his commitment to overcoming adversity and past hurts. Pastor John Lindell loves God, and he's been my pastor for over 30 years. He and his wife, Debbie, are part of my team. Gal Gadot, well, she's on my team. I mean, she takes good care of herself, and that inspires me. Just saying.

Who are the influencers in your life? Who are you following on social media? Who are you listening to? Who do you spend precious time with? This is critical. Who are you allowing to have a voice in your life? It's a big deal. Your team will influence your life. Research has shown that if you spend a significant amount of time with a friend who emulates unhealthy habits, it will change your perception of healthy habits, and your behavior will change accordingly.[24] Surround yourself with people who have habits you want to aspire to. "Do not be misled: Bad company corrupts good character" (1 Cor. 15:33). It goes the other way, too. If you spend your time with friends who are happy with their lives, you are 6 percent more likely to be happy yourself. Be intentional about the people you're allowing in your life. Spend time with God, with family, with a mentor/friend, and with people who inspire you. This is your team.

BIBLE COLLEGE

I knew I had a calling on my life, like we all do. I was eighteen and seeking the Lord for direction with my future. My youth pastor spoke often about Bible College. I wasn't sure that was the path for me. I graduated high school, got a great job at a financial lending institution, and began to make good money. I deposited my checks and began to think about my financial goals. I had it all figured out. My first purchase was a new sports car. My next purchase was going to be an expensive, beautiful coat. Then, I was going to buy myself a large diamond ring. This was the order of my wish-list.

I worked very hard. Then, one day, out of nowhere it hit me. This was not what God had called me to. I got home one night and told my parents that I believed I needed to go to Bible College. My parents were supportive but not really sure what to do next. No one in my immediate family had ever gone to college.

It was time to make a decision. I had already missed the fall semester while I was making millions at my job (just kidding; it felt like millions to me). The college route would involve spending money, not making it. Aye aye aye! I needed to hear from God on this. The deadline for the spring semester was the following day. I went to bed and prayed, "Lord, I don't know what to do. I need to hear from you if this is the path I'm to take. Please give me a peace in the direction I'm supposed to go. If I feel peace in my heart to go to college, I will go. If I feel more peace about working, I will keep working. I will pray through the night, as long as it takes, because I must make a decision by tomorrow." I prayed, and prayed, and prayed some more. The next thing I knew, I opened my eyes and it was morning. The moment I opened my eyes, I knew beyond a shadow of a doubt that I was supposed to go to Bible College. I felt the peace that I had been praying for.

I applied to Bible College. I filled out my paperwork and tried to figure out what classes to take and how to apply to live on campus. Soon after, I received a letter of acceptance and it was time to start packing. It all went so fast. I began school in January for the spring semester. There were a couple of things I had to do now that my life was going in this direction.

The first thing was to break up with a boyfriend that I liked very much, maybe even loved. I felt that God wanted me all-in, and I couldn't have any distractions as I was seeking His will for my life. It broke my heart to end the relationship, but I was on a mission, and I felt like that was part of my journey. I felt I was supposed to be solo at this particular moment in my life, so I cut all ties.

MARRIAGE AND MISCARRIAGE

Long story short, I attended Bible College that spring and the following fall semester. I was discovering where I felt I would be working in ministry. I studied education and missions. It was during my missions-studies that I met a boy. He was studying to be a missionary, and after dating for nine months, we married. I was 20 and he was 23. We had been married for three years when I became pregnant with our first baby. We couldn't believe it. We were so excited. My mom and dad came to visit and we went shopping. We bought everything you could possibly need for a baby's room. I was elated. We purchased everything in white, so it wouldn't matter if it was a boy or girl.

I was just starting to wear my new maternity clothes and the unthinkable happened. I miscarried my baby at 11 weeks. It all happened so fast. One minute I was thinking about names, and the next minute I was getting cards from everyone telling me they were "sorry for my loss." It was almost surreal. It never crossed my mind that my baby wouldn't make it. My bedroom looked like a florist. I didn't want to be sad. I remember lying in bed and processing what had just happened. It was in that moment that I thanked God for His sovereignty and told Him that I would always trust Him on this journey. I wanted to believe that God had a different plan for my baby, and His plan was always the best plan.

A year went by, and then I cried. I was driving down the highway and tears filled my eyes. I was finally mourning the loss of my first baby. I cried for a bit and then dried my eyes. I know God loves me. I know God knows what's best. I made up my mind to trust God's plan over my ability to understand the ways in which He works.

My Sweet Boys

Three years later, God blessed me with a beautiful baby boy weighing 9 pounds, 10 ounces and 23 inches long. That baby is now 25 years old and six-foot-four, and he has the kindest heart of anyone you could ever know. Two-and-a-half years later, God gave me a second precious son who is now 22. All his life, his demeanor was so gentle I would get tears in my eyes when I'd talk to him. Both of my sons bring me more joy than I could ever put into words.

Speaking of joy, there was that lovely day we were driving home from the store when the boys were probably 8 and 10 years old. I looked over, and they had just opened my brand new lighter I bought to light the grill and my candles. Apparently, they wanted to see how long it would take to melt the Wal-Mart sack. Thankfully, screaming and flailing the bag in the air put the fire out in no time.

Adventurous little guys they were, I tell you. There was that time the boys had friends over and they were excited to set off fireworks in the front yard. I was in the house and noticed the boys walking quickly through the house with two little drinking cups, one in each hand. I followed them to the front door to see flames coming up from the yard. All of the boys were doing everything they could think of, including stomping on the fire and melting their tennis shoes. I grabbed the water hose and we were able to extinguish the flames. I can honestly say I don't recall ONE boring day with my little blessings. Not one. They brought laughter and fun every day of our lives.

CHOOSE JOY

In the English Standard Version of the Bible, the words joy, rejoice, or joyful appear a total of 430 times. This is God's plan for you. Anything less is not from Him. Everyone is sad at times, but that is a temporary feeling. We allow ourselves to mourn loss, but there is a time when God whispers, Okay, I'm healing your heart and it's time to live again, because I have much more for you. That was just a season. Choosing joy is a real thing. God has a plan just for you, a beautiful plan that will bring you joy, if you choose. Joy is a strong emotion. It comes from God, and His joy will actually make you strong. "The joy of the Lord is your strength" (Neh. 8:10). If you're going through a season and you need joy, ask God for help. Start giving Him praise for your blessings and soon joy will fill your heart. His joy will overwhelm your soul and carry you through every season of your life.

Obstacles

Henry Ford once said, "Obstacles are those frightful things you see when you take your eyes off your goal." Obstacles can be anything. There can be obstacles keeping you from a closer walk with God. Obstacles keeping you from growing as a person. Are there some things that are keeping you from your goals? One of the first steps in gaining momentum is elimination. Are there distractions that need to be eliminated so that you have a clear path to your goals?

Make one big move in the direction you want to take your life. Your power move may mean canceling appointments in your week that keep you too busy for time with God. Remove extras in your life that are distractions from your goals. While I was writing this paragraph, my phone alerted me that a friend was asking me to meet this evening. I politely declined. I'm currently on a mission to write a little book — this one. It is my priority at this time in my life. Gary Blair calls it "crossing the Rubicon, reaching the point of no return."[25] That is where I am. I heard from God, and my heart is to obey Him. That is a decision we all get to make. I have a resolute drive that keeps me focused in order to accomplish what I feel God has called me to do.

"Oh, magnify the Lord with me" (Ps. 34:3, ESV). As you magnify the Lord, He's your focus and you are not magnifying anything else. Whatever you're magnifying is king. Keep your focus on God, so you don't lose sight of His mission. When asked how they define success, many great athletes answer, "focus." I love the story of one of the most famous home runs in World Series history that occurred on October 1, 1932. The score was tied, and Babe Ruth was up to bat. He famously pointed to the outfield before he hit the ball exactly where he pointed and ran his amazing home run, which helped to win the World Series. That move, pointing to the outfield, still inspires people today. It was bold. It was audacious. It was focused. Interestingly, the jersey that "The Babe" wore the day he called that shot was sold at auction in 2005 for $940,000.[26] Success follows focus.

Rid yourself of obstacles, and bravely focus on exactly where you want your life to go. Obstacles can be negative relationships. Be so busy with your positive relationships you don't have time for the less supportive and crippling ones. Maybe you need time alone, maybe an hour or a day or a weekend, but get alone with God until you have clarity on your next step to take. Put a little space between you and anyone who doesn't share your vision. Distance from people making poor choices will help you keep your laser focus and avoid negativity in your life. Be so busy being the best you for God that nothing will diminish your zeal for the things God has put on your heart.

Action Step:

Take a look at the people you follow on social media. Clean up your feed. Maybe it's time to rethink anything or anyone who doesn't share your joy and desire for wholeheartedly following after God. Fill your feed with good news, Scripture, positive stories, and the things that inspire you. Start following people who walk with God, people who post wise words filled with encouragement and truth. Find podcasts of people who work hard and are mastering subjects you want to know more about. Prepare for a positive influx of information. Everything you consume will be nutrition for your life. Growth will be inevitable.

Day 15

GRATITUDE

It's not happiness that brings gratitude.
It's gratitude that brings happiness.

Your past. The good, the bad, the ugly — have all played a role in shaping the strong person you are today. What would happen if you looked back at every single experience with gratitude? I know what you're thinking: You don't know what I've been through. You don't know how bad it was. You're right, I don't. None of us know one another's stories in depth. We just know that we all have a story. What if we chose to be grateful for our stories instead of angry or hurt? Grateful that we survived. Grateful that it changed. Grateful that we are now strong. Grateful that we learned. Grateful for growth. You will know you've grown when you can honestly become grateful for your story. When you choose to be thankful, you will be sitting in the driver's seat. This will be your strength. This is our last power move.

You will have an infinitely richer life when you train yourself to write healthy stories about your life events. One of my all-time favorite comeback stories is Joseph (Gen. 37-50). Wow, I'm getting teary-eyed as I write. This guy; he was so strong, so mentally tough. Do you know how? He walked with God and chose gratitude. Remember his life of incredibly unfair treatment? He had been sold as a slave, beaten, left for dead, and imprisoned for a crime he didn't commit. His past was not fair, not one bit of it. In the end, the tide turned. His story changed. He, like Esther, ended up in a palace.

Maybe you feel like your life hasn't been fair. Joseph was in prison for something HE DIDN'T DO. "The Lord was with him; and whatever he did, the Lord made it prosper" (Gen. 39:23). You may be in a season of feeling imprisoned. Look around you. If you look closely, you will see that God is right there with you, just like He was with Joseph. Don't look at the injustice, look for God in your story.

Ten of Joseph's brothers went to Egypt for help. The brothers traveled to meet with the overseer of the land, not realizing it was their little brother, Joseph. They did not recognize him. He spoke through an interpreter so they wouldn't know he could understand when they were talking to one another. Joseph had to turn his head from them at one point to weep. He was so hurt, but even in his pain he forgave them. They begged for food for their families. Again, Joseph was overwhelmed, so much so that this time he had to dismiss himself and go to his room to cry. Then, he washed his face and came back to talk to the brothers. Do you see Joseph's humanity? He had to process the pain, just like we do. He had to navigate forgiveness, just like we do. He had to love through the pain, just like we do.

"Then Joseph said to his brothers, 'Come close to me.' When they had done so, he said, 'I am your brother Joseph, the one you sold into Egypt! And now, do not be distressed and do not be angry with yourselves for selling me here, because it was to save lives that God sent me ahead of you'" (Gen. 45:4-5). Joseph trusted that God had a bigger plan for his life. He was now in the palace and was the second in command. God had given him favor on the other side of countless, seemingly hopeless situations.

We can never go wrong when we keep a soft heart. God will reward hard work, humility, and kindness.

> "But God sent me ahead of you to preserve
> for you a remnant on earth and to save your
> lives by a great deliverance. So then, it was not
> you who sent me here, but God. He made me

father to Pharaoh, lord of his entire household and ruler of all Egypt." ... "You intended
to harm me, but God intended it for good
to accomplish what is now being done, the
saving of many lives. So then, don't be afraid.
I will provide for you and your children."
And he reassured them and spoke kindly to
them (Gen. 45:7-8; 50:20-21).

Mind blown. This man wrote his own story of love, a story of courage, honor, and valor. He owned his past. He was a victim at the hands of no one. His life had greater purpose. He forgave the people who wronged him, and then he went a step further. He reassured the villains and abusers and spoke kindly to them. How about that for a challenge? Never speaking words of defeat over our pasts ever again, but choosing only kindness, forgiveness, and love? The decision is ours. We choose the story we want to write. Choosing gratitude will speed the healing process. What was meant to harm us God will use to strengthen and empower us. Can you imagine a heart so tender that you forgive the ones who tried to kill you? Joseph said that it was all part of God's plan to save all of them. That story is for us today. As we keep our hearts soft and stay close to God, watch for His leading, and we will experience His provision and healing.

Trust God in the depths of hardship. He never fails. Trust His perfect plan and perfect timing. Take the time to intentionally reprogram your thoughts to be grateful for your past. Get alone with God and He will help you grow in gratitude. God will give you a healthy, hope-filled heart.

A Grateful Grannie

A 92-year-old, petite, well-poised, and proud lady, who was fully dressed each morning by 8 a.m., with her hair fashionably coifed and makeup perfectly applied, even though she was legally blind, moved to a nursing home. Her husband of 70 years had recently passed away, making the move necessary.

After many hours of waiting patiently in the lobby of the nursing home, she smiled sweetly when told her room was ready. As she maneuvered her walker to the elevator, her caretaker provided a visual description of her tiny room, including the eyelet sheets that had been hung on her window. "I love it," she stated with the enthusiasm of an eight-year-old having just been presented with a new puppy.

"Well, Mrs. Jones, you haven't seen the room. Just wait."

"That doesn't have anything to do with it," she replied. "Happiness is something you decide on ahead of time. Whether I like my room or not doesn't depend on how the furniture is arranged; it's how I arrange my mind. I already decided to love it. It's a decision I make every morning when I wake up. I have a choice. I can spend the day in bed recounting the difficulties I have with the parts of my body that no longer work, or get out of bed and be thankful for the ones that do. Each day is a gift, and as long as my eyes open, I'll focus on the new day and all the happy memories I've stored away, just for this time in my life."

What a beautiful story. Could anything be truer of our thoughts? We get to decide every single one of them. No one else gets to do that for us. Make a good choice today. What an incredible gift, the gift of choice. Choose a grateful heart. As you are creating a healthy you, speak words of life and gratitude over yourself and every story that involves you. Encourage and inspire your world with your own words. Speak words of courage and strength. Speak truth. "I have a kind heart. I work hard. I love a big life. I am thankful for my life. I am blessed beyond measure. I love to dream. I love God. I am choosing to trust God with my whole life." Remind yourself of God's promises. Quote Scriptures that strengthen you. "I am fearfully and wonderfully made" (Ps. 139:14). God has "plans to prosper [me] and ... to give [me] hope and a future" (Jeremiah 29:11). Write your favorite verses where you will see them and be reminded of God's truths. Memorize Scripture so that you can quote it throughout your day when the enemy comes against your thought life. Make sure your conversations are faith-filled and pleasing to the Lord. Every word that comes out of your mouth is either life or death. Choose life. Choose gratitude.

Like the 92-year-old woman who had already decided she loved her apartment, decide you already love your life, your future. It's a decision. How exciting is that? As Henry Ford once said, "Whether you believe you can or can't, you are right." Recognize the power of your words and thoughts over your life. You have the power of decision.

MY PINK JOURNEY

I was alone, sitting in the so-very-quiet doctor's office. I was holding back tears. The nurse had gone to get help because she couldn't stop the bleeding from the breast tissue biopsy they had just done. She let me know that if the bleeding didn't stop soon, they may have to send me to the Emergency Room. You see, two weeks prior, I was diagnosed with breast cancer. On this particular day, they were doing a next level biopsy. As I was sitting in that room, my head was still spinning because I couldn't believe I had been diagnosed with breast cancer. There I was, 48, and no one in my family had ever been diagnosed with breast cancer. In fact, there wasn't any history of cancer in my family. What in the world? I felt like I was in a daze. And then, out of nowhere, I could hear faint music playing over the sound system that I hadn't heard before in the room. Tears came to my eyes when I realized it was one of my favorite songs by MercyMe, "Grace Got You". The lyrics talk about dancing, even in the rain. Don't let your smile leave you. You can dance because you know God's grace has got you.

I looked up and smiled as if God was right there in that room, and I whispered, "Thank you. I believe you've got me. Thank you, God." I don't want to be too graphic, but I was losing quite a bit of blood. Then, it stopped. They had to clean the room, the floor, the table, my clothes, and my shoes. Now it was time to talk through the next several weeks of surgery and radiation treatments.

What a journey. I heard phrases like, "You have one of the fastest growing cancers, but you caught it early" and, "We will begin radiation 30 days after your last surgery." Not exactly the lingo I thought I'd ever hear pertaining to me. God was so good to me through all of it. He gave me a faith like I had never had. I was confident that He was in control, and that made me feel safe, no matter the outcome.

A few weeks into my radiation treatments, I got a phone call from the hospital asking me if they could publish my story in their medical newsletter and post it to their media sites because my story was somewhat unique. You see, I had been to the doctor. There were no lumps, no symptoms, nothing.

My doctor happened to ask if I'd had my annual mammogram. I answered, "Oh yes, I did that a few years ago."

He smiled and said, "You really need to get that scheduled, Marla." That was it. His nudging never left me.

Several weeks went by, and I finally scheduled that mammogram (mostly so my doctor's voice in my head would go away). Mammogram day came. I had a cousin coming through town, and she called and asked me to meet for lunch. I was looking for any excuse not to go to my appointment. I met her and her family and watched the time. Oh yay, it looked like I was going to have to reschedule. I called the doctor's office and said, "I'm so sorry, but I'm running so late. I think I'll have to reschedule."

"Well, how late will you be?" the nurse asked.

"At least 30 minutes or more," I responded.

She said, "Well, why don't you still come. We will make it happen."

I persisted. "Oh, I can totally reschedule so you don't have to wait for me."

"We can wait," she replied. "You just come as soon as you can."

What in the world? This was not what I expected to hear. So, I headed to the cancer center for my awesome mammogram.

I checked in at the desk, and sat in the waiting area. After a while, they finally called my name. I sat in a little cubicle with the office assistant, so we could discuss the procedure and the cost. I had great insurance with my work, but after the nurse stopped talking, I just looked at her and said, "Ma'am, I know this may sound crazy, but can I cancel this appointment?"

She looked at me for a minute and said, "Um, yes, you can."

"Thank you so much," I replied. "I will be sure and call you if I have any symptoms. I will definitely do that."

"Okay, no problem," she said.

Feeling really bad, I said, "Thank you so much. I hope this wasn't a huge inconvenience." She was very kind, and we both stood.

I picked up my purse, and turning to walk away, I heard the voice of someone dear to me, "You were right there. Why didn't you just do it? You were already there."

I turned to see the nurse about to leave the desk and said, "Excuse me, ma'am. I'm so sorry. I'm here; I think I better just do this."

She smiled and said, "Are you sure?"

I wanted to say, "Please, for the love of Pete, don't ask me that. Let's just get this over with!" Instead, I smiled and said, "Yes, ma'am."

I went back to the medical rooms and had the mammogram done. I then had to go to the waiting area while they looked over the findings. My name was called, and I was asked to go back a second time. That's when they sent me to a small room labeled "Consultation." I started to get a little fidgety and began to pray. I started repeating to myself, "Everything is okay, it's going to be okay, it's okay." I also began to say, "Thank you, Lord, for my journey. I know you have a wonderful plan." Then the door opened, and it wasn't a nurse, it was a doctor.

He sat down in front of me, kind of close, and said, "Marla, we have found something that isn't right." My heart sank. I was pretty sure they had the wrong file, until he said, "Are you okay?"

I just sat there. I said, "Do you mean you think I might have cancer?"

"I'm saying that there is a possibility," he replied. "Your work has come back, and there is definitely something there that, yes, could be cancer." I was just quiet. I didn't know what to say. "Do you have any questions for me?" he asked.

"No, sir," I answered. "Thank you for telling me."

He asked, "Are you sure you're okay?"

"Yes, I'm okay; it's okay."

He told me which desk to go to next, but I didn't really hear one word he said. It was like in the movies where you see their mouths moving but it's all muffled. I remember getting in the car and heading home. I was trying to process what just happened.

The cancer center was amazing and acted quickly. I was assigned a nurse for my cancer journey. She would call and check on me and let me know my next scheduled procedure, etc. It was the longest two months of my life — so many doctor visits, surgeries, and procedures. I remember so clearly an unexplainable peace that God had given me. Just like that song said, "grace had me." I had already decided that God had a good plan, whether it would be through my life or through my passing. Every day, I would thank and praise Him for my journey, no matter what it looked like. I was thankful I didn't have to worry because God had told me, "Do not fear." I had resolved to hold tight to Him and let Him lead me on this path of trust.

A week went by after the first surgery, and the nurse called me. "Marla, the measurements have all come back, and we didn't get the clear margin we needed around the place the cancer was removed. We need to schedule another surgery."

Honestly, I felt like I had been holding it together pretty well, until that moment. I began to cry. "Okay, no problem. When is my next surgery?" Soon after that call was surgery number two. I'm sharing some details about this journey so that you understand, I had to make up my mind more than once to choose joy. Repeatedly, I had to choose to trust God. I had to choose peace. I had to choose hope.

Then, it was time for radiation treatments. "You will come to this office every day for your radiation treatments for the next four weeks." Oh my! I remember the first time I walked back and there were huge signs hanging every-where: "RADIATION," "HAZARDOUS RADIATION," "WARNING! RADIATION!" I had to lie on a big table a certain way so that the radiation laser beams would hit the right spot. They positioned me on the table and said, "Okay, we'll be right back." Everyone would leave the room. I would lie there alone in that big white room. All of the machines would start up and move around my table. I could see red lasers aiming from every direction. This was my life every weekday for a month.

I became really good friends with the radiation tech-nicians. I was so happy to invite several of them to church. I prayed that God would use my story to encourage the workers I met along the way. I prayed that He would use my joy and peace to show them that He can calm any storm we encounter. God did many beautiful things during those weeks. I'm thankful I was able to share Jesus with an office full of new friends.

Two months had gone by since my diagnosis, surgery, and radiation. I loved the staff, but I was so happy to say goodbye to this cancer journey. I was waving goodbye to everyone on my last visit, and a nurse followed me down the hall. She said, "Are you ready to ring the bell?"

I was like, "What bell?"

She said, "Your victory bell. You did it! You beat cancer!"

I was like, "OH!" I wasn't quite sure what to say, so I said, "Oh, that's okay. I'm just happy it's all over." I was by myself, so there wasn't really anyone to cheer. I didn't know what to do.

My sweet nurse wouldn't hear of it. She said, "Let me see your cell phone." She held it up and said, "Now you just ring that bell." So, I did.

Walking to my car that day felt a little different than all the other times. The air was fresher. My life felt sweeter. I think I took a deeper breath than I ever had before. I began to cry and just thank God for His hand on my life, and for His love and His care on that journey. It was a wonderful day.

A thankful heart strengthened me on that journey, I know it. Every time I would thank the Lord for an unknown future, I would feel a supernatural peace and joy that words fall short to describe. God wants to carry our weight. Whatever weight you're carrying, He says, "Cast all your anxiety on Him because He cares for you" (1 Peter 5:7). He means that. He wants you to trust Him fully with your life. He wants you to rest knowing that He has a plan, He hears your prayers, and He loves you deeply. No matter what your journey looks like, it's going to be okay. In fact, it's going to be wonderful. You have the Creator of the universe, the Almighty God, at the helm of your life. "Trust in the Lord with all your heart, lean not on your own understanding, in all of your ways, submit to Him and He will make your paths straight" (Proverbs 3:5-6). Trusting God and submitting to Him is peaceful. You can trust Him to clear your paths and steer you in the right direction. Trust Him more than you trust your ability to make sense of it all.

How Do You Want to Show Up?

Decide how you want to show up for life. Ask God to give you wisdom to know how to pray specifically for this. If you have a certain reputation that you don't like, change it — today. You can reinvent yourself right now. You know the saying, "You are one decision away from a totally different life." Only one person can make that happen for you. You. Whatever you feel prompted to work on, research the Scriptures that pertain to who you want to be. Grow in these areas. Study to develop the characteristics you want to encapsulate. The door is wide open for you to become whomever you desire to be.

You have the power to decide how you will show up to the dinner table, to work, and to church. Make your decision. Follow through with positive, encouraging, and life-giving words to empower yourself to succeed. Decide when you wake up, decide before you walk in that door, decide before you go to that meeting. You have the ability to show up any way you'd like. That is refreshing. Love the person you are becoming.

NEVER, NEVER, NEVER GIVE UP

One day you will thank yourself for not giving up and always showing up. No matter how hard it is, show up with a smile. Be an encourager, even when it's challenging. As you inspire others, you will be inspired yourself. Whatever you want to be — kind, gentle, loyal, hard-working, dependable, trustworthy — all of it is possible starting right now. Ask God for help. He will expedite your journey. Do the hard work today, and reap the benefits for a lifetime.

God cares about every season of your life, the almost-too-good-to-be-true seasons and the crazy-hard ones. "The Lord draws close to the brokenhearted and saves those who are crushed in spirit" (Psalm 34:18). When you're hurting, God is close to you. He sees your pain, and He's about to save you. He's going to mend your broken heart. You are His favorite creation, made in His image. Trust His timing to work out every detail of your situation.

MY TEACHER'S NOTE

By the time I was nine years old, I seemed to get more spankings for dishonesty than anything else. In my heart of hearts, I cannot think of a single instance where I intentionally lied, but through a series of misunderstandings, this became a thing in my life. When I was in third grade, there was a situation in my class. The teacher asked who in the room had left a book out when we went to recess. I walked up to her desk and said, "That was me." She thanked me for coming to her, and I went back to my desk. Later that day, I found a note on my desk that read, "Dear Marla, Thank you for being so honest. Now I know I can always trust you, Ms. Sharon." I took that note home and hung it on the wall next to my bed. I read it almost every day of my childhood years. I read it until I believed it. That teacher gave me a new name. She called me honest. She changed the trajectory of my life. I would no longer accept that I was dishonest. I had proof that I was an honest girl. How powerful was that note? That was several decades ago, and I still remember every word of that note and still have it in a keepsake box.

"Do not withhold good from those to whom it is due, when it is in your power to act" (Proverbs 3:27). "Good" includes good words. Speak encouragement. You have the ability to share the gift of encouragement and change someone's life forever. Share the joy of hope with everyone you meet. I can think of no greater ministry than speaking powerful, encouraging, life-giving words over others and, yourself. Gentle, kind, and uplifting words will inspire hope. The hope this world so desperately needs. How exciting to think of entering heaven and seeing the lives that we touched throughout our lifetime. The people we unknowingly spread hope to through kind words or a smile. The small acts and words of encouragement at just the right time and changed the trajectory of someone's life.

It's a Jeep Thing

After one of the hardest seasons of my life — you know, the one where you think you're going to die, but you didn't — I did a thing. Some girls go shopping, some girls consider taking up permanent residency in a chocolate factory, and then there's me. I decided to fix up my cute little white Jeep Wrangler. I'm a firm believer in loving your vehicle, especially if one of your favorite pastimes is taking road trips (like me).

Talk about, "Um, where did all my money go?" I mean, it was fun but, oh my, can those super cool upgrades add up! I asked a friend of mine to pick out brands, styles, and what he thought would look best. (Note to self: don't ask a guy who's never entered a lifted Jeep in five-inch heels to pick out your lift kit). The day came, and I went to pick her up. She was so cute with all the new bling, and then there was the moment I had to get in. You see, my friend had put a 3¼-inch lift and 35-inch tires on my cute little baby. For all my girlfriends, let me explain. Imagine jumping on a horse in stilettos. Need I say more? Eventually, I did nail it.

After all the upgrades, it came time to name my little diva on wheels. I knew immediately what to name her. I went straight to a local vinyl sign shop and placed an order for my new Jeep name to be put on both sides of the hood. I looked at the guy at the sign shop and said, "Help! My Jeep looks like a dude's Jeep! You gotta help me. I need the scrolliest, girliest, font you have for the hood." He did it! Written in beautifully-scrolly black letters on the white hood of my now girly Jeep was her new name, HOPE. I got a little teary-eyed and wanted to tell the sign guy my whole story (because I know how men love to chat while they're at work and have a line of customers waiting), but I didn't. I did feel like I needed to explain the tears, so I simply said, "Yeah, I just got on the other side of cancer." He was so sweet. He looked me in the eye and said, "That's a big deal. That's awesome. Congratulations."

As I drove away, I imagined someone sitting at a stoplight going through something really hard. They would look out their window and see my Jeep, and then they would see it: HOPE. I pray that everyone who reads the hood of my

Jeep would be inspired to keep hoping and never give up. Try one more time! Everything is going to work out! Keep going! Don't quit! God still has a plan!

ANSWERING THE CALL

Is there something God has been stirring in your heart? Perhaps it's time to have a serious conversation with the Lord about the desires He's placed in your heart. Maybe you're considering writing a book, strengthening a relationship, going for a promotion at work, leading an event, volunteering, studying something you're passionate about. Ask the Lord to open doors and He will. Ask Him to multiply your time and He will. If God has spoken, obey right away and watch the blessing that follows. Blessing always follows obedience.

YOUR TURN

Now it is time to implement these habits and make them part of your everyday life, never looking back. You will begin stacking one goal, one dream, one miracle at a time. You will see a pattern of victory because you made a decision to live differently. You chose life. You chose dreams. You chose hope. Live your life for God, and trust Him with the details, the parts of your story that you don't have answers for at this moment. Start right now. Prepare for an empowered life that only God can orchestrate. He loves to answer your prayers because He loves you deeply. "See what great love the Father has lavished on us, that we should be called children of God" (1 John 3:1). As you live for God, He will guide you and bless you. Ask Him for wisdom, and He promises to give it freely. He will order your steps. "The steps of a good man are ordered by the Lord: and He delighteth in his way" (Psalm 37:23, KJV). He goes before you. You can walk in confidence, believing that He will answer your prayers. "For the Lord God is a sun and shield; the Lord bestows favor and honor; no good thing will He withhold from those who walk uprightly" (Psalm 84:11, ESV).

Defeating the discouraging whispers of the enemy will be a battle you will win as you go. Recognize his ploy to steal your hope and prepare to conquer. Memorize every Scripture we've talked about, and you will get stronger with every trial. Keep the Word of God in your heart, ready to remind the enemy of his place, and get back to the Father's business. With any setback, you will notice your recovery time is shorter and shorter, and you will take a deep breath and watch God "equip you with strength for the battle" (Psalm 18:39).

Use the tools and Scriptures in this book every time you need to be reminded that God has very intentional and purposeful plans for you. Keep in mind that the enemy wants you to believe anything but that. You may be in a season of preparation. Learn in this season. Get stronger in this season. "Do not despise these small beginnings, for the Lord rejoices to see the work begin" (Zech. 4:10). Slow and steady wins the race. Accomplish your goal, and then move to the next one.

I don't know what spreading hope looks like for you. Maybe it means baking cookies for a neighbor, or paying for someone's coffee behind you, or sending a text, or writing a book or sharing this one? Maybe sharing hope looks like you cheering on and lifting the arms of someone who's taking a huge leap of faith. Supporting and praying for him or her. Sometimes sharing hope is a smile.

Here's to your new adventure! The Bible refers to new beginnings and a new day and the mercies of the Lord are new every morning. Today is a new day filled with hope and promise. There will be amazingly beautiful moments, and seasons that you will be in a spiritual battle for your life. Never fear, you have all that you need — hope in God.

I prayed every day for you as I was writing this book. I prayed that God would give you supernatural insight and confidence in Him. He is your rock and your provider. As long as you walk close to Him, you win. You will not go through one trial that God will not equip you to handle. Stand firm in knowing that God loves you and He is for you. Don't run after the wrong things. Be intentional with your time. God will bring you all that you need for your journey, and at just the right time. And while there are seasons of growth and challenges, as you spend time with God, you will be strengthened specifically for your journey. "My flesh and my heart may fail, but God is the strength of my heart and my portion forever" (Ps. 73:26).

Action Step:

Fill your life with hope. Do your part. Don't look to your right or to your left; keep your laser focus on God. Run after Him. Do everything He reveals in black and white (His written Word), and your life will be most blessed, as He promised. He will turn your story into the most beautiful story if you let Him. "May the God of hope, fill you with all joy and peace in believing, so that by the power of the Holy Spirit you may abound in hope" (Romans 15:13, ESV).

Gratitude

HOPE ALWAYS WINS NOTES

Introduction

1   Abigail Johnson Hess, "51% of Young Americans Say They Feel Down, Depressed or Hopeless—Here's How Advocates Are Trying to Help," CNBC, May 10, 2021, https://www.cnbc.com/2021/05/10/51percent-of-young-americans-say-they-feel-down-depressed-or-hopeless.html?&qsearchterm=Abigail%20Johnson%20Hess%20depressed.

2   "Blood Vessels," The Franklin Institute, accessed April 2021, fi.edu/heart/blood-vessels.

3   "Dr. Benjamin Hardy Talks Personality Isn't Permanent and Habits, June 17, 2020, https://www.linkedin.com/pulse/benjamin-hardy-talks-personality-isnt-perma-nent-lane-kawaoka-pe#:~:text=There's%20actually%20a%20good%20quote,you%20didn't%20learn%20enough

4   George Couros, "Beyond Knowing," georgecouros.ca, 2021, https://georgecouros.ca/blog/archives/6701.

5   Pierce Marrs, "If You're Not Growing, You're Dying," The Sales Moment, Issue 247, August 1, 2016, https://pierce-marrs.com/blog/.

6   Dr. Benjamin Hardy, June 16, 2020, "Break Free from Self-Limiting Beliefs with Dr. Benjamin Hardy" https://www.youtube.com/watch?v=4bBZfU6Bka4

7   Dan Sullivan, "10 Laws of Lifetime Growth," accessed April 2021, https://resources.strategiccoach.com/the-multiplier-mindset-blog/the-laws-of-lifetime-growth.

8   Paul Napper and Anthony Rao, "The Power of Agency," November 4, 2020, https://waiyancan.com/summary-the-power-of-agency-by-anthony-rao/.

9   Dr. Benjamin Hardy, June 16, 2020, "Break Free from Self-Limiting Beliefs with Dr. Benjamin Hardy" https://www.youtube.com/watch?v=4bBZfU6Bka4

10 Martin Luther King, Jr., "Martin Luther King, Jr Quotes," accessed April 2010, https://www.keepinspiring.me/martinluther-king-jr-quotes/#more-2655.

11 Justin Taylor, "A Woman of Whom the World Was Not Worthy: Helen Roseveare," December 7, 2016, https://www.thegospelcoalition.org/blogs/justin-taylor/a-woman-of-whom-the-world-was-not-worthy-helen-roseveare-1925-2016/

12 Luke Bradshaw, "Olympic Heroes: Karoly Takacs and His Wait for Gold," December 29, 2016, https://theculturetrip.com/europe/hungary/articles/olympic-heroes-karoly-takacs-and-his-wait-for-gold/

13 James Clear, "Forget About Setting Goals. Focus on This Instead," accessed June 28, 2021, https://jamesclear.com/goals-systems.

14 Heather Craig, "The Research on Gratitude and Its Link with Love and Happiness," accessed May 2021, https://positivepsychology.com/gratitude-research/.

15 Admiral William McRaven, "Make Your Bed: Little Things That Can Change Your Life...and Maybe the World," August 17, 2017, https://www.youtube.com/watch?v=3sK3wJAxGfs

16 Libby Sanders, "The Case for Finally Cleaning Your Desk," Harvard Business Review, March 25, 2019, https://hbr.org/2019/03/the-case-for-finally-cleaning-your-desk.

17 Craig Groeschel, "Praying Through the Pain: Anxious for Nothing," Life Church, accessed May 2021, https://www.life.church/media/anxious-for-nothing/praying-through-the-pain/.

18 Olivia Blair, "Using the Word Stress Less Could Actually Make You Less Stressed," April 20, 2017, https://www.independent.co.uk/life-style/health-and-families/

word-stress-using-less-make-less-pressure-mental-health-work-relationships-anxiety-a7692641.html

19 Gary W. Keller and Jay Papasan, The ONE Thing: The Surprisingly Simple Truth Behind Extraordinary Results, (Austin, Texas Bard Press) 2013.

20 Dr. Benjamin Hardy, " How To Achieve 10x More Than Your Peers" Florida, https://www.youtube.com/watch?v=8HD_uwHzcjQ

21 "Wayne Gretzky," Wikipedia, accessed April 2021, https://en.wikipedia.org/Wayne_Gretzky.

22 "Wayne Gretzky Quotes," accessed April 2021, https://www.brainyquote.com/quotes/wayne_gretzky_383282

23 Laura Reiley, "The Sky is Falling for Fast Food, but not for Chick-fil-A. Here's Why," The Washington Post, June 19, 2019, https://www.washingtonpost.com/business/2019/06/19/chick-fil-a-becomes-third-largest-restaurant-chain-us/.

24 David Burkus, "You're Not the Average of the Five People You Surround Yourself With," mission.org, May 2018, https://medium.com/the-mission/youre-not-the-average-of-the-five-people-you-surround-yourself-with-f21b-817f6e69.

25 Gary Blair, "The Rubicon — A Master Class from Julius Caesar," April 24, 2020, https://medium.com/

mind-munchies/the-rubicon-a-master-class-from-julius-caesar-e9fe736b332e.

26   "Babe Ruth's 'Called Shot' Jersey from the 1932 World Series," Robb Report June 25, 2021, https://robbreport. com/shelter/art-collectibles/slideshow/10-most-valu-able-baseball-world-series-collectibles-all-time/1-babe-ruths-called-shot-jersey-from-the-1932-world-series/

CPSIA information can be obtained
at www.ICGtesting.com
Printed in the USA
LVHW050004241021
701304LV00006B/7